Words Begin in Our Hearts

Words Begin in Our Hearts

WHAT GOD SAYS ABOUT WHAT WE SAY

Rhonda Rizzo Webb

MOODY PUBLISHERS
CHICAGO

Library of Congress Cataloging-in-Publication Data

Webb, Rhonda Rizzo, 1963-
   Words begin in our hearts : what God says about what we say / by Rhonda
Rizzo Webb.
      p. cm.
   Includes bibliographical references and index.
   ISBN 0-8024-3415-0
   1. Oral communication—Religious aspects—Christianity. 2. Interpersonal
communication—Religious aspects—Christianity. I. Title.

BV4597.53.C64W43 2003
241'.672—dc21

                                                                    2003001327

1 3 5 7 9 10 8 6 4 2

Printed in the United States of America

To Mama and Daddy
The beauty of your hearts is evident in your
words of Life and encouragement to me.
Thank you.

Contents

· · · · · · · · · · · · · · · ·

Introduction

W hen I tell people that I have written a book about what God says about what we say, they instantly clam up. They become sheepish about speaking in my presence for fear they might say something "wrong." So I try to put them at ease. I'm certainly no language saint on a rampage! Rather, I'm a kindred spirit, a Christian woman who, because of my own failures to control my tongue, has resolutely sought God's Word to find hope, not judgment. Instead of loading others down with guilt, my aim is to offer inspiration and practical methods for pursuing godliness in the way we speak.

A few years ago, while leading a ladies' Bible study, this matter hit me like a ton of bricks. Although I had been a Christian for more than twenty-five years, I realized that I was completely oblivious to what God's Word really said about how I am to master my mouth. One of our directives during this particular study was to discuss the material to our hearts' content—but not at our husbands' expense. I knew that Scripture said not to slander anyone, yet before this sudden enlightenment, it had seemed permissible to tell unflattering stories about my husband, Jimmy.

Coloring our husbands in a not-so-attractive light is contrary to what God would have us do, yet our culture encourages it. It's not only socially acceptable, but it's kind of fun and, well, downright expected. This realization stunned me. The world *does* enforce behavior that opposes God's Word. (Okay, so that might not be news to you.) I began seeing how this is true in so many areas of life, but especially in reference to my words.

The information in this book really applies to both men and women, in fact, to believers of all ages. It is addressed primarily to women, however, because I am a woman who has seen the fruit of controlling my tongue (although I have not mastered it). This is a process, and pursuing it has not only lifted my self-respect, but it has also increased the respect and trust others have for me. And I haven't turned into an old fuddy-duddy or party pooper, like I feared, but just the opposite, it seems.

This experience reminds me of Daniel, who refused Babylon's wisdom and clung instead to doing what he knew was right before God. How did people respond to him? Did his friends shun him or the royal guard throw him into a dungeon? No. He became more powerful and more popular, second only to the king (Daniel 1–2).

The more we Christians reject the world's wisdom and strive to do God's will, the more attractive our lives will become to nonbelievers—and the more our lives will glorify our Father. Choosing God's ways over the world's ways should be a no-brainer for us!

My desire for you is that this book will give you a new vision for how God's Word is real and alive today. I pray that the time you invest in studying what God says about what you say will encourage you in applying biblical truth to your daily walk . . . and *talk!*

> *She opens her mouth in wisdom,*
> *And the teaching of kindness is on her tongue.*
>
> Proverbs 31:26 (NASB)

Where Did That Come From?
Wrong Words Begin in Our Hearts

. . . .

*"For out of the overflow of the heart
the mouth speaks."*

MATTHEW 12:34

When my son, Jimmy, was four, he was *constantly* talking. "Mama. Mama. Mama. Mama." One afternoon while driving down a country road near our home, Jimmy would not stop chattering. I finally cracked, slammed on the brakes, and told him that if he did not stop talking for five minutes, I would leave him on the side of the road. Well, he quieted down. I drove about five feet and stopped the car again. At this point we were both crying. I climbed into the backseat, held his hands, told him how sorry I was for speaking to him that way, and asked him to forgive me. It broke my heart to think that my son might for a fleeting moment think I would ever desert him.

Where did that outburst of angry, hurtful words come from? Have you ever been utterly shocked by the words that seem to come pouring out of your mouth without any warning? Have you been surprised to hear foul language pass through your lips before you even knew it had formed on your tongue? How does that happen?

God's Word says that our mouths speak out of the overflow of our hearts:

> *"Make a tree good and its fruit will be good, or make a tree bad and its fruit will be bad, for a tree is recognized by its fruit. You brood of vipers, how can you who are evil say anything good? For out of the overflow of the heart the mouth speaks. The good man brings good things out of the good stored up in him, and the evil man brings evil things out of the evil stored up in him. But I tell you that men will have to give account on the day of judgment for every careless word they have spoken. For by your words you will be acquitted, and by your words you will be condemned."*
>
> Matthew 12:33–37

The word *heart* in verse 34 is the Greek word *kardia*. It refers to our thoughts, motives, feelings; our will; and our character. *Kardia* also implies the "center." Thus, our hearts represent our whole inner person. Who we are inside overflows through the escape hatch of our mouths. When we are growing in godliness, the evidence of that growth will flow from the center of our beings and out through our mouths as godly words. However, if we are not turned toward God, what else can flow from us but that which is not honoring to Him?

In the NASB, Matthew 12:35 reads, "The good man out of his good treasure brings forth what is good." Treasure is the Greek word *thēsauros*, which has at its root the word *tithēmi*, which means "to place." Whatever we place in our hearts is what we have to "bring forth." We have the responsibility and the power to place or store up either virtue or evil in our hearts.

OUR WORDS REVEAL OUR CHARACTERS

"What goes into a man's mouth does not make him 'unclean,' but what comes out of his mouth, that is what makes him 'unclean.' . . . But the

things that come out of the mouth come from the heart, and these make a man 'unclean.' "

Matthew 15:11, 18

In this confrontation with the Pharisees, Jesus made it plain that a purely outward religion which ignored the condition of the heart was not pleasing to God. What defines a person is what fills his or her heart, and this is revealed by what comes out of his or her mouth.

Do you get the point that every time we open our mouths to speak, we are uncovering our characters? Baring our souls to the world? By means of the words we speak, everyone who hears can recognize precisely the kind of people we really are. This can be frightening! Just that thought is enough to make me want to whip myself into shape. But how?

A CHRIST–CENTERED HEART

A Christ-centered heart is foundational for producing godly communication. That's why I put this chapter first. In my experience, the sooner we understand how to develop a Christ-centered heart, the sooner our lives and words will begin to reveal godly character. From Psalm 119:10–12 I have derived three steps to achieving a Christ-centered heart:

> *I seek you with all my heart;*
> > *do not let me stray from your commands.*
> *I have hidden your word in my heart*
> > *that I might not sin against you.*
> *Praise be to you, O LORD;*
> > *teach me your decrees.*

1. Seek God through genuine prayer for a righteous heart.

2. Fill your heart with God's Word.

3. Train yourself for the purpose of godliness.

Let's look at each step one by one.

Seek God Through Genuine Prayer for a Righteous Heart

In 1 Kings 3:1–15, God came to Solomon and said, "Ask for whatever you want me to give you." Solomon's request is in verse 9: "Give your servant a discerning heart to govern your people and to distinguish between right and wrong." God was so pleased that Solomon had not asked for a long life or riches but for a discerning heart that He gave Solomon what he asked—and then added riches and honor besides!

If God told you, "Ask of Me the one thing you desire most, and it will be yours," what would you ask for? Would your request match Solomon's—a righteous, discerning heart? That's what we need most, isn't it? A heart that can discern between right and wrong, a heart that honors God.

If our hearts aren't discerning, what are they? God's Word calls them "hardened." When Jesus refers to hardness of heart, He is picturing hearts that have become spiritually unperceptive and insensitive (see Mark 8:17). But this condition doesn't have to be permanent. Ezekiel gives us hope for change:

> *"I will give them an undivided heart and put a new spirit in them; I will remove from them their heart of stone and give them a heart of flesh. Then they will follow my decrees and be careful to keep my laws. They will be my people, and I will be their God."*
>
> Ezekiel 11:19–20

If we ask Him to, God will take out our stony, deadened hearts and replace them with tender, responsive hearts "of flesh." God will renew our hearts when we genuinely desire clean hearts. The key is *genuine* desire, as Solomon had. We have to really mean it when we pray for a new heart. This inevitably requires giving up things that have become significant to us, such as having our way and our familiar routines and patterns. In order to fill our hearts with Christ and His righteousness, we must empty them of all the ungodly garbage that so often fills them—things like selfishness, arrogance, and unforgiveness.

For example, consider my friend Tina and her husband Greg. Greg was dishonest with Tina throughout their entire marriage, and she forgave him time and time again. But finally, she just couldn't take it anymore and packed up the children and their belongings and went to live with her parents. She felt so hurt and betrayed that she feared bitterness would take root in her heart. While Greg went through hours of counseling and was held accountable by a select group of godly men, Tina and the kids stayed away, separated from him indefinitely.

Tina asked for prayer for her heart, asking God to soften her and make her receptive to a changed Greg. She feared that anger, hurt, and resentment toward him would take over and characterize her; yet she also feared that if she let go of those things, Greg would just hurt her again. Tina could have put her trust in her anger and hurt as the means for Greg's needed reformation, but would this really have changed him? No, only God and Greg could do that. If she wanted to be free to forgive Greg and learn to trust him again, she would have to be willing to let go of her bitterness, hurt, and resentment and trust that the new heart the Lord would give her was more than worth the risk.

In order to experience God's power in our hearts, we must be willing, as Solomon was, to give up or lay aside the things that seem most important to us. You've heard the phrase, "Let go and let God." That is what we must do if we truly want a righteous heart.

The words of King David are still the perfect and timely petition for us today:

> *May the words of my mouth and the meditation of my heart*
> *be pleasing in your sight,*
> *O LORD, my Rock and my Redeemer.*
>
> Psalm 19:14

Fill Your Heart with God's Word

Once we have turned our hearts over to God, we are ready for the next step. Phase two in the transformation of the heart is to fill our hearts with God's words:

> *I have hidden your word in my heart*
> *that I might not sin against you.*
> Psalm 119:11

The Hebrew word used here for *hidden* means "to treasure, hide, protect, hoard, reserve." This same word is used in Exodus 2:2, when Moses' mother hid him from Pharaoh's army for three months. God's Word should be as precious to us as the baby Moses was to his mother!

When our hearts and minds are filled with the treasure of God's Word, we have also gained a powerful weapon. Remember when Jesus was tempted by Satan in the wilderness? Jesus responded to every temptation by quoting Scripture: "It is written . . ."

Satan first suggested to Jesus, who had been fasting for forty days, that He turn the nearby stones into bread. But Jesus replied with Deuteronomy 8:3, "It is written: 'Man does not live on bread alone, but on every word that comes from the mouth of God'" (Matthew 4:4).

Next, Satan challenged Jesus to prove He was God by throwing Himself off the pinnacle of the temple and letting the angels catch Him. But Jesus answered using Deuteronomy 6:16: "It is also written: 'Do not put the Lord your God to the test'" (Matthew 4:7).

Finally, Satan offered Jesus power over the world if only He would bow down and worship him. But Jesus replied from Deuteronomy 6:13: "Away from me, Satan! For it is written: 'Worship the Lord your God, and serve him only'" (Matthew 4:10).

How do we get God's Word into our hearts as Jesus did in His? It takes time and commitment. We must spend time in Scripture for it to become part of us. I can suggest four specific ways to prompt this result: (1) regular personal Bible study, (2) Scripture memory, (3) group Bible study, (4) Bible-based books.

Regular personal Bible study. While growing up, I was taught that you must have a quiet time first thing in the morning, every morning. Well, I am not much of a morning person, and if I missed a day, I felt so guilty I could hardly function.

Having daily Bible study first thing in the morning is an incredible discipline for which I still strive. However, the time of day is not as important as actually doing it. As a mother, I would like to have my devoted time in God's Word first thing in the morning. But if my son wakes up extra early and prohibits my study time, it works out well for me to study God's Word during his naptime. As a professional woman, I spent many lunch hours in the car at the park in Bible study. If you get coffee breaks at work, why not spend them in God's Word? If you like to read before going to bed at night, why not read God's Word instead of mail-order catalogs? Let me encourage you to not get so hung up on the time of day or the number of minutes. Just do it!

You can accomplish effective daily Bible study in several ways. Many people use a system that suggests certain passages of Scripture to read each day that will allow them to complete the entire Bible in a year. I use two different approaches: book study and word study. In book study, I choose a book of the Bible and read it through several times, each time digging deeper into its meaning. I use a concordance, several versions of Scripture, and other study guides to help me understand the context. I write my thoughts and questions in a journal and cross-reference until I am satisfied that my questions are resolved.

In word study, I choose a word, like *heart,* and try to find out everything that Scripture says about that particular word, again using different versions of Scripture, concordances, and other study materials. I journal my findings and write how these conclusions apply to my life. Each of these types of study can take weeks in which to weary myself, although I am confident I will never exhaust God's Word.

There are assuredly other methods of personal Bible study. The key is to find a method that excites you and through which you can absorb God's Word into your life.

Scripture memory. As part of your regular study time, you should incorporate Scripture memory. That is how you, too, will be able to respond to temptation with, "It is written . . ."

You can memorize Scripture in many ways. In college, my friend Alicia had a little Lucite box attached to the dash of her car. In it were several small cards with verses printed on them. She would memorize Scripture on the long drive between the university and her home on the weekends. My friend Val writes out verses that she needs to memorize on 4 x 6 index cards and keeps them in her kitchen so she can look at them regularly. I keep index cards in my study next to the computer, because I am there frequently. When I worked in an office, these index cards were tacked to the bulletin board at my desk. Gideons International provides their members with a small, folding, wallet-like packet that holds cards imprinted with Scripture that can be carried easily in a pocket or handbag. A Bible study in which I participated a few years ago suggested that if you have difficulty memorizing Scripture, you should write out the verse you wish to learn ten times. By the time you are done, you know it.

Again, find a method that works for you. Whether you memorize a verse a month, a verse a week, or a whole book of the Bible, you are making progress in filling your heart with God's words.

A great place to start your Scripture memory would be using the verses quoted in this book. Write them on index cards and put them where you can go over them frequently. Once you know them, whenever you are tempted to participate in unwholesome speech, you can respond with, "It is written . . ."

Group Bible study. The church I attend has a strong emphasis on small group Bible studies. We have several groups of a dozen or so people who meet together frequently for in-depth Bible study. My husband and I meet with a group of about twelve men and women on Wednesday nights in our home. We often study a specific book of the Bible using a workbook or study guide. This is an incredible opportunity for us to study together. The group also provides a wonderful forum for discussion.

If your church doesn't offer small group Bible study, many towns have community Bible study programs, or perhaps another church in your area does have small groups. If you can't find either of these, start a Bible study group of your own. During the summer, our church usually does not offer a formal women's Bible study program. So a friend and I invite some other ladies and have our own group study for the summer. This past summer we studied prayer using Kay Arthur's *Lord, Teach Me to Pray* and Bruce Wilkinson's *The Prayer of Jabez*.

Bible-based books. I strongly encourage everyone I meet to read Bible-based nonfiction books. Whether it is a book about losing weight or about raising children, if it incorporates Scripture within the text, it will help you incorporate Scripture into your everyday life. Many books are available that have opened up God's Word to thousands of people by helping them apply Scripture to their health, to raising children, to having a successful marriage, and even to organizing their closets. All the books I have read by Kay Arthur or Beth Moore have amazed me at how God's Word so perfectly applies to my life today.

These are all merely suggestions. Other ways to get God's Word into your heart include learning and singing Scripture-based songs like "He Who Began a Good Work in You," which is based on Philippians 1:6. Many other effective avenues for hiding God's Word in your heart are available. The point is to begin *today* to actively pursue that goal, so when you are tempted to communicate in an ungodly manner, you can respond with, "I have hidden your word in my heart that I might not sin against you" (Psalm 119:11).

Train Yourself for the Purpose of Godliness

Have nothing to do with godless myths and old wives' tales; rather, train yourself to be godly.

1 Timothy 4:7

Paul was instructing Timothy to avoid "worldly fables fit only for old women" (NASB). This refers to fables being taught as truth in that day that mixed Christianity and paganism.[1] Isn't it interesting that Scripture contrasts participating in this type of ungodly talk with disciplining yourself for godliness?

Martha Peace, in *The Excellent Wife,* calls this training a "process of diligence." It takes work. She points out that the New Testament Greek word for *discipline* is *gumnazō,* which means "to exercise or train." In other words, it means to do it over and over until you get it right. The English word *gymnastics* comes from this Greek word. How godly we become depends on how hard we work at it, how hard we exercise. "Old habits of sinful thoughts and responses do not just disappear. They have to be replaced with new, godly ways of thinking and responding."[2] As Paul wrote:

> *We take captive every thought to make it obedient to Christ.*
> 2 Corinthians 10:5

> *Do not conform any longer to the pattern of this world, but be transformed by the renewing of your mind. Then you will be able to test and approve what God's will is—his good, pleasing and perfect will.*
> Romans 12:2

As we take our ungodly thoughts captive (grab them before they get out of our mouths), then replace them with godly thoughts and comments, eventually the godly response becomes the automatic response.

SUMMARY

Our words reveal our character. Those words come from the overflow of our hearts. God's Word tells us that what we put into our hearts is what is recycled into our words. We have the responsibility and the power to alter our hearts. We must decide that having a righteous heart is the most important objective by asking God, first and foremost, to give us a new heart. Then we can ultimately transform our hearts by filling them with God's Word—hiding His Word in our hearts. Finally, we must be continuously training ourselves for the purpose of godliness by diligently capturing sinful thoughts, feelings, and motives and replacing them with new, godly ways of thinking and responding.

～2～
Was That the Wrong Thing to Say?
Defining Ungodly Words

. . . .

Do not let any unwholesome talk come out of
your mouths, but only what is helpful for
building others up according to their needs,
that it may benefit those who listen.

EPHESIANS 4:29

What is unwholesome talk, anyway? The King James Version calls it "corrupt communication." The word *corrupt* suggests rottenness, like rotten fruit. Yet that still doesn't answer the question. How about defining the opposite of unwholesome talk? According to Ephesians 4:29, the inverse of unwholesome talk is language that is helpful, that builds up, that meets needs, and that benefits others. If our speech does not meet these requirements, then it can most likely be defined as unwholesome, corrupt talk.

Have you ever placed the requirements set in Ephesians 4:29 on your own words? Ask yourself these questions: (1) Do my words help? (2) Do my words build up? (3) Do my words meet needs? (4) Do my words benefit others?

In our community, we are good friends with several couples.

Some of the husbands hunt, fish, and ski together; and when they go on their manly outings, the wives often get together for "girls' night" to watch romantic movies and visit. I specifically recall the conversations from some of those girls' nights a few years ago.

As we were eating our fancy hors d'oeuvres and sitting cross-legged in the den in our sweats with vanilla-scented candles burning and *Sleepless in Seattle* playing on the VCR, we inevitably got to talking about our husbands. "The other day Scott did so-and-so." The rest of us giggled, gasped, muttered "Men," or all three. Another of the girls would pipe in, "Scott is an angel compared to Danny. Last week he . . ." (Again, giggle, gasp, "Men.") Then another, "What are they thinking?" Yet another, "Robert is exactly the same. Just Thursday night I thought I would strangle him when he . . ." "Well you won't believe what Doug did. This outdoes them all!" (Giggle, gasp, "Men.")

This would go on for hours. It never occurred to me that this conversation might not be pleasing to God. It was just fun, innocent girl talk, or so I thought.

Then, a little over a year ago, while leading a women's Bible study on becoming a godly wife, I realized that I had been tearing down my husband. One of the directives during this study was to encourage the participants to share about the material but never at their husbands' expense. We are called to slander *no one* (Titus 3:2). So why do we think it is justifiable to tear down the most important men in our lives?

Suddenly, it dawned on me. Modern culture, even the church, says it is acceptable to complain about your husband's behavior. Gracious! Some call it venting, which is only healthy, right? Some call it innocent girl talk. But God's Word calls it slander. *Slander* in Scripture means defamatory statements about another. Any statement that paints another in a not-so-flattering light is slander, according to Scripture.

What if I had asked myself the four questions posed in Ephesians 4:29 as requirements for biblical speech?

1. Does it help another when I slander my husband? Well, it might make a few girls giggle, but really, the answer is no. It hurts my husband's reputation. It belittles him in the eyes of my girlfriends.

2. Does disparaging my husband build others up? No. It actually tears down my husband.

3. Does it meet another's needs? No.

4. Does it benefit others? No. It only encourages my girlfriends to criticize and find fault with their husbands and to be less satisfied with their marriages.

Wow. How many other unwholesome words does our culture advocate? The following pages will identify, but probably not exhaust, other areas of speech that may be socially acceptable or even applauded in our society, but which are contrary to God's Word and His will for our lives.

Let's look at Scripture passages that specifically identify areas of speech that are contrary to God's will. We will define each type of speech; classify it as careless, crafty, or corrupt; then contrast culture's opinion with the biblical view of each category of communication. You'll soon discover that our society considers wrong speech acceptable in one form or another. While extremes may be taboo or distasteful even in worldly circles, many of these elements are applauded and admired. It is in the subtle uses of these types of words that Satan deceives us and tarnishes our characters.

CARELESS WORDS

Anger

What is it? The Greek word refers to violent passion, punishment, and loss of self-control. Parents can easily spot anger in the way they discipline or correct their children. Many parents find themselves screaming at their children in anger before they even realize it. "How many times do I have to tell you?" Many are at a point of feeling, "This child just isn't going to grasp the lesson unless I yell and scream!"

Speaking in anger is classified as careless because when we speak in anger, we are not thinking of the consequences of our words. We are not in control of our words at all but letting the emotion of the moment boil over in our speech.

What is culture's opinion? In many instances, the world encourages us to express everything we feel. If we feel anger, we should express it. It is healthy to vent. Yet it is really Satan who tells us that the listener just won't get it unless we express ourselves in anger.

What is the biblical view? Colossians 3:8 says we "must rid" ourselves of anger. This implies that we do have control over it. Thus, there is no excuse for a loss of self-control. Self-control is a fruit of the Spirit (Galatians 5:23). Proverbs 19:19 says that a man of anger will pay a great penalty. And listen to what James tells us:

> *My dear brothers, take note of this: Everyone should be quick to listen, slow to speak and slow to become angry, for man's anger does not bring about the righteous life that God desires.*
>
> James 1:19–20

Since the ultimate goal of correcting our children is their righteousness, our anger is a fruitless waste of energy. The same applies to situations involving adults. When we express ourselves in anger to our spouses, another adult, or a child, we should not expect to achieve the righteousness of God. In other words, our anger is not going to fix anything.

Complaining and Grumbling

What is it? *Webster's* defines the word *complain* as "to express grief, pain, or discontent,"[1] but its synonym *grumble* is more the idea of what God counsels against: "to mutter in discontent."[2] Why does the Lord view grumbling so seriously? Because what it really reveals is disbelief, a rejection of how God has provided for and led us. Such "murmurings oppose faith and will soon destroy it."[3]

What is culture's opinion? Complaining is just another acceptable form of communication in our world. We've all heard, "Nobody likes a complainer," yet everyone still complains about everything. We complain about the government. We complain about taxes. We complain about the service at a restaurant. We complain about the quality of entertainment available on television and at the movies. We complain to our husbands that they don't fix the washer, change the toilet paper roll, or put the seat down.

What is the biblical view? James makes it crystal clear:

> *Don't grumble against each other, brothers, or you will be judged. The Judge is standing at the door!*
>
> James 5:9

If you think you accomplish anything positive by complaining or nagging, God's Word says otherwise. By complaining, you just put yourself in judgment's way. Nowhere in Scripture does it say that complaining stirs up faith or godly action. On the contrary, the immoral, condemned false teachers that Jude rebukes are also characterized as "grumblers and faultfinders" (Jude 16). God has a different path He wants His children to travel:

> *Do everything without complaining or arguing, so that you may become blameless and pure, children of God without fault in a crooked and depraved generation, in which you shine like stars in the universe.*
>
> Philippians 2:14–15

We are to do *everything* without complaining. Our goal in life is not to get everything "off our chest" but to become blameless, pure children of God without fault. God promises that we will shine like stars in the universe. In my opinion, the results of not complaining vastly outweigh the alleged benefits of doing so! What do you think? My friend John often says, "You can whine, or you can shine!"

Foolish Talk

What is it? Foolish talk is heedless buffoonery. It is inconsiderate and thoughtless. Foolish talk refers to words that are spoken without thought for how they will affect another.

What is culture's opinion? "Sometimes you just need to be goofy." "You can't protect everyone's feelings all the time." "If something you say seems inconsiderate to someone else, that person is just being too sensitive." "You need to speak your mind." "People think too much." Do any of these statements sound familiar to you?

What is the biblical view? Ephesians 5:4 says this kind of talk is out of place among followers of Christ:

> *Nor should there be obscenity, foolish talk or coarse joking, which are out of place, but rather thanksgiving.*

Instead of being thoughtless, we are to honor others above ourselves (Romans 12:10). In other words, another's feelings and needs are much more important than expressing our frivolous thoughts.

Wrath

What is it? Wrath is a higher level of anger or rage. It is fierceness or indignation. Indignation is defined as righteous anger or "anger aroused by something unjust." When I think of wrath, I envision protesters at an abortion clinic shouting at clinic employees. Wrath is taking anger to an extreme level.

What is culture's opinion? You are a hero in many circles if you express indignation or righteous anger. The more flamboyant, fierce, and creative you are in expressing your indignation, the more you are admired. Many people, including many Christians, encourage this type of communication in protest against some political issue that is considered against God's laws. Many in our culture express this level of wrath at sporting events. Referees and umpires receive special training to deal with such violent outbursts.

What is the biblical view? Ephesians says we are to lay aside wrath (4:31). If we are going to protest against something unjust, wrong, or counter to God's Word, expressing ourselves in wrath cannot possibly be a productive method. As the old saying goes, "Two wrongs don't make a right."

CRAFTY WORDS

Arrogance

What is it? Contemptuous, cocky boldness and disregard for others are the characteristics of arrogant speech. It lacks respect for others, as well as simple modesty. When we speak arrogantly, we often belittle and talk down to others, usually in a condescending tone of voice.

I once worked with a fellow named Charles who didn't have a terribly high view of women. His speech made this very apparent. To one of his female peers he might bark, "Hey, honey, how about a cup of coffee, black." One day, Charles was called on the carpet for his arrogant attitude. His response was, "I really didn't mean to sound condescending." Then turning to the ladies in the room, he said, "Oh, I'm sorry, girls, do you know what 'condescending' means?" That is arrogance!

What is culture's opinion? The world might call this kind of attitude "self-confidence." Arrogance is admired in many circles. In the business world, for example, a cocky attitude may help you get ahead.

What is the biblical view? First Samuel 15:23 says that arrogance is "like the evil of idolatry." In many ways, arrogance is evidence that people idolize themselves or their public image. Wisdom hates arrogance (Proverbs 8:13). Arrogance will not go unpunished:

> *The arrogance of man will be brought low*
> *and the pride of men humbled;*
> *the LORD alone will be exalted in that day.*
>
> Isaiah 2:17

> *I will punish the world for its evil,*
> *the wicked for their sins.*
> *I will put an end to the arrogance of the haughty*
> *and will humble the pride of the ruthless.*
>
> Isaiah 13:11

God's Word tells us that in order to be a leader, one must first be a servant. Humility, the opposite of arrogance, is praised in Scripture (James 4:6) and is outward evidence of a Spirit-filled life (Matthew 5:5).

Bitterness

What is it? Bitterness is a poison of the soul. *Webster's* defines *bitter* as "galling; exhibiting intense animosity, harshly reproachful, marked by cynicism and rancor."[4] Bitterness finds expression in sharp, cutting remarks and sarcasm. Bitter words differ from words of malice in that they stem from anger and unforgiveness taking root in our lives. The resulting harsh remarks are usually directed toward the person considered the cause of our pain or troubles.

What is culture's opinion? When this type of emotion is expressed via sarcasm or piercing remarks, it is revered in our culture. As I was growing up, being witty was a must. All of my good friends were so sharp and funny. I had to work at being humorous so I could fit in, and it seemed that sarcasm made other people laugh. I practiced one-line zingers just so I could be as clever as my pals were.

In the 1980s, the popular television drama *Dynasty* featured two lead female characters, Alexis and Crystal. These two unbelievably beautiful women would meet at an elegant dinner party adorned in sparkling diamonds and lavish designer evening gowns. Their conversation would consist of cruel, venomous insults hurled one after another, each uttered through perfectly painted, smiling lips, with impeccable grammar and inflection, each punctuated with fluttering, false eyelashes. High society and picture-perfect as it was, it was still bitter talk.

What is the biblical view? James 3:14–15 says that the "wisdom" that finds bitterness attractive is of the devil:

> *But if you harbor bitter envy and selfish ambition in your hearts, do not boast about it or deny the truth. Such "wisdom" does not come down from heaven but is earthly, unspiritual, of the devil.*

Ephesians 4 says, "Get rid of all bitterness" (v. 31). Obviously, we should want to eliminate anything that is of the devil from our lives. The book of Hebrews gives us another reason why we should rid our lives of bitterness:

> *See to it that no one misses the grace of God and that no bitter root grows up to cause trouble and defile many.*
> Hebrews 12:15

Bitterness just ends up causing trouble and corrupting others. I don't know about you, but I certainly don't need trouble, and I absolutely do not want to miss the grace of God!

Boasting

What is it? Boasting is talking proudly. We often call it bragging. When a person babbles on about her accomplishments, material possessions, or abilities, she is boasting. When she constantly drops the names of important or influential friends in regular conversation, she is boasting.

What is culture's opinion? The world says no one is going to think higher of you than you do of yourself, so make sure other people know how important you are. Self-esteem is a priority in our culture. "You can't get ahead without tooting your own horn."

What is the biblical view? James writes that boasting is evil:

> *Now listen, you who say, "Today or tomorrow we will go to this or that city, spend a year there, carry on business and make money." Why, you do not even know what will happen tomorrow. What is your life? You are a mist that appears for a little while and then vanishes. Instead, you ought to say, "If it is the Lord's will, we will live and do this or that." As it is, you boast and brag. All such boasting is evil.*
>
> James 4:13–16

God is the one who gives or takes away. Our abilities and possessions are gifts from Him. If we must boast, we should boast of the mercy of our God (Jeremiah 9:23–24).

Gossip

What is it? A gossip is one who spreads rumors. Gossiping includes telling secrets, often very personal ones. Women in the church, unfortunately, are notorious for gossiping. A group prayer time often becomes an opportunity to gossip; it's just disguised as piously requesting prayer for another. If, when you talk, you find yourself needing to look around to see who is near enough to hear—you are probably gossiping. If you feel the need to speak in a hushed tone of voice or to partially cover your mouth while talking, you are probably gossiping.

What is culture's opinion? We love to talk about juicy tidbits of other people's lives. Entire television programs and magazine publications are dedicated to gossip. A recent article in *Psychology Today* magazine even says that gossip is good. Apparently, evolutionary psychologists have discovered that the human race has adapted in such a way that gossip is now an important part of our survival and fulfills important functions in civilized society.

The article cites three important functions of gossip: (1) Networking. This is interaction that allows us to jockey for social position. (2) Influence. Having privileged information to share gives us influence with others and is tied up with our need to promote ourselves. (3) Alliances. In these associations, "People supply information to whom they are attracted and with whom they wish to align themselves." While we form these alliances to suit our advantage, we also put those being gossiped about at a disadvantage.[5]

What is the biblical view? Scripture views gossip as harmful: "A gossip separates close friends" (Proverbs 16:28). And Paul confessed to the difficult Corinthians:

> *For I am afraid that when I come I may not find you as I want you to be. . . . I fear that there may be quarreling, jealousy, outbursts of anger, factions, slander, gossip, arrogance and disorder.*
> 2 Corinthians 12:20

Paul also links gossiping with being a busybody (1 Timothy 5:13). Is that how we want to be identified? Proverbs 20:19 also tells us to avoid a person who talks too much. That person is a gossip and will betray a confidence. Romans 1:29–31 connects gossip with wickedness. What do you believe—God or *Psychology Today?*

Lying and Deceit

What is it? To deceive is to lie or attempt to mislead another. Deceit is tricky and sly, scheming to misrepresent the truth.

What is culture's opinion? If it is just a "little white lie," it is acceptable, fine even. When lying is necessary to protect another or to keep us out of trouble, our culture views it as really no big deal.

What is the biblical view? In John 8:44, Jesus describes Satan, the greatest evil in existence, as "a liar and the father of lies," adding that "there is no truth in him." To lie, then, is to turn against the truth and ultimately against God, because the Lord is a God of truth—truth is part of His very nature (see Psalm 31:5; Isaiah 65:16). As Christians, we no longer have the nature of Satan but the nature of Christ. Therefore, lying is no longer part of our "native tongue" and should be like a foreign language to us. Notice the things with which God associates lying:

> There are six things the Lord hates,
>   seven that are detestable to him:
>   haughty eyes,
>   a lying tongue,
>   hands that shed innocent blood,
>   a heart that devises wicked schemes,
>   feet that are quick to rush into evil,
>   a false witness who pours out lies
>   and a man who stirs up dissension among brothers.
>   Proverbs 6:16–19

Does that sound like "no big deal"? Deceit is not only unacceptable, it is a deadly sign of hate: "A lying tongue hates those it hurts, and a flattering mouth works ruin" (Proverbs 26:28).

Malice

What is it? Malice is defined as depraved, evil, and injurious communication. It is the desire to see another suffer. Communicating with malice is using words that deliberately hurt the listener. Like the proverbial playground bully mockingly calling the little girl with glasses "four eyes," so adults often use their words to hurt or insult others. The motives that prompt malicious talk are crafty and impure.

A popular television series a few years ago was *Designing Women*, which featured a character, Julia Sugarbaker, who had the sharpest tongue in the South. She could cut anyone down to size with a few whips of her skilled lips. I remember looking forward to the show just to see if she got any juicy, lacerating lines that night. Oh, how I wished I had the capability (or at least the writers) to use my tongue as such a formidable weapon.

What is culture's opinion? It is hard to imagine that our culture would encourage such a hurtful thing. Yet, have you ever been told to defend yourself, to verbally strike back, to injure the other person at least as much if not more than he or she has hurt you?

What is the biblical view? Unfortunately, the God I serve wasn't too thrilled with my desire to use my tongue as a weapon. First Corinthians 5:7–8 tells us to eliminate the yeast of malice and wickedness. First Peter 2:1 says, "Rid yourselves of all malice." Titus 3:3 includes malice as part of the life we lived when we were too foolish to know any better. Instead of defending ourselves with wicked words, Scripture tells us to return kindness to those who would harm us (Luke 6:27). God's Word tells us to rid ourselves of malice completely. It does not say to keep a little malice around just in case it is really warranted in a given situation. No inkling of malice has any place in our Christian walk.

Slander

What is it? Slander is tearing down another person's reputation. Webster's defines it as "the utterance of false charges or misrepresentations which defame and damage another's reputation."[6] Slander is crafty because it is so deliberately harmful to others.

What is culture's opinion? Though we may criticize it, the tabloids and nearly every political campaign are rife with slander—and these methods work in our society. Why else do those papers sell, and why else do politicians keep using those mudslinging ads? Because they make money, and they get votes.

What is the biblical view? The writer of Proverbs says that "whoever spreads slander is a fool" (10:18). Psalm 101:5 warns, "Whoever slanders his neighbor in secret, him will I put to silence." Christians are commanded to never slander anyone:

> *Remind the people to be subject to rulers and authorities, to be obedient, to be ready to do whatever is good, to slander no one, to be peaceable and considerate, and to show true humility toward all men.*
>
> Titus 3:1–2

Slander is behavior in which we may have participated when we were foolish and deceived (v. 3). Now that we are saved and renewed (v. 5), however, we are beyond such things. So let's get rid of it. Let's not allow slander to be part of our lives (Ephesians 4:31).

Strife

What is it? Strife in Scripture means debate, contention, or quarreling. It is incessant, divisive arguing.

What is culture's opinion? "You must fight for what you believe in." "Stand your ground." "Don't let other people walk all over you." How often have we heard statements like these?

What is the biblical view? Scripture says that causing strife is evil and wicked (Romans 1:29–31). And Proverbs makes these observations:

> *It is better to live in a desert land*
> *Than with a contentious and vexing woman.*
> Proverbs 21:19 (NASB)

> *It is to a man's honor to avoid strife,*
> *but every fool is quick to quarrel.*
> Proverbs 20:3

> *Starting a quarrel is like breaching a dam;*
> *so drop the matter before a dispute breaks out.*
> Proverbs 17:14

Instead of starting a quarrel, or even continuing one, we should abandon it quickly before it gets out of hand and does damage we can't undo.

CORRUPT WORDS

Blasphemy

What is it? Blasphemy is treating the Lord with contempt,

insult, or irreverence. This includes but is not confined to taking God's name in vain.

What is culture's opinion? Culture says it is impossible to truly express yourself without the use of these words. It is especially expected among men and in the business world. Our culture also considers it cool and effective to use blasphemous slurs, which can be seen every time we turn on the television, even in prime time, and are bombarded by this kind of talk. Movies have become so pimpled with obscenities and the mocking of God that we don't even seem to notice it anymore.

What is the biblical view? The Bible calls blasphemy misusing God's name and tells us to cast it aside. As our Lord said in the third Commandment:

> *"You shall not misuse the name of the* Lord *your God, for the* Lord *will not hold anyone guiltless who misuses his name."*
> Exodus 20:7

If you doubt the Lord's seriousness, Leviticus 24:16 should clear it up for you: "Anyone who blasphemes the name of the Lord must be put to death." Did Jesus lessen the severity in the New Testament? Here's what He said:

> *"I tell you, every sin and blasphemy will be forgiven men, but the blasphemy against the Spirit will not be forgiven. Anyone who speaks a word against the Son of Man will be forgiven, but anyone who speaks against the Holy Spirit will not be forgiven, either in this age or in the age to come."*
> Matthew 12:31–32

The Lord's name and character are holy, and as His people, we should be as protective of them as He is.

Cursing, Filthy Communication, and Coarse Joking

What is it? Cursing is speaking evil of or against others, desiring to hurt them or tear them down, often with offensive language.

Filthy communication refers to vile conversation or shameful talk, including any language that would be considered off-color or not appropriate in mixed company. Coarse joking is vulgar, indecent humor. Many times, these types of discourse include references to sexual sin or some other type of perversion, often punctuated by crudeness and obscenity.

What is culture's opinion? It is exciting to talk about things so vile that they make your skin crawl or that push the limits of our comfort level. And what's a comedy routine without sexual or bodily function references? Jerry Springer and Howard Stern still have a sizable enough audience to remain on television, it's sad to say.

While working in the technology industry, one of my associates, Joe, could hardly breathe a sentence without the use of at least one expletive, and usually several. I often felt beat up after merely discussing the weather with him. This behavior apparently wasn't too offensive in our culture, for Joe was an incredibly successful man in what many consider a very tough and competitive industry. He had one of the most sought-after jobs in the business and retired a multimillionaire by the age of fifty. Consequently, it seems our culture rewards filthy language.

What is the biblical view? God calls it prudent, not prudish, to refrain from such talk. Paul again says, "Rid yourselves of all such things" (Colossians 3:8). Filthy, depraved talk is a characteristic of the person who doesn't know God, whose thoughts are futile, and whose heart is darkened. Cursing and filthy, coarse communication are a result of turning one's back on God. To participate in such language is contradictory for a Christian, as James wrote:

With the tongue we praise our Lord and Father, and with it we curse men, who have been made in God's likeness. Out of the same mouth come praise and cursing. My brothers, this should not be. Can both fresh water and salt water flow from the same spring? My brothers, can a fig tree bear olives, or a grapevine bear figs? Neither can a salt spring produce fresh water.

James 3:9–12

SUMMARY

All of these ways of speaking are obviously contrary to the way Christians should communicate. Now that we know them, we are accountable for getting rid of them. How in the world can we remember all of these areas? It seems overwhelming. What is left? Is there any kind of "right" speech available to me? Yes! In fact, almost every Scripture passage listed in this chapter is surrounded by verses listing godly alternatives for our words. We will look at them in depth in chapter 3 and throughout the remainder of this book.

While the list in this chapter may not be exhaustive, we can always refer to the requirements for wholesome speech found in Ephesians 4:29:

> *Do not let any unwholesome talk come out of your mouths, but only what is helpful for building others up according to their needs, that it may benefit those who listen.*

And remember to ask yourself: (1) Do my words help? (2) Do my words build up? (3) Do my words meet needs? (4) Do my words benefit others?

As godly women, I believe we are called to ensure that our speech follows these guidelines. How much more effective for the Lord we can be when we do. Why don't you pray today that the Father would help you identify those areas of your life and alert you before any wrong speech passes through your lips? Pray Psalm 19:14:

> *May the words of my mouth and the meditation of my heart*
> *be pleasing in your sight,*
> *O LORD, my Rock and my Redeemer.*

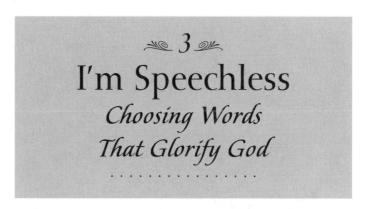

I'm Speechless
Choosing Words That Glorify God

No temptation has seized you except what is common to man. And God is faithful; he will not let you be tempted beyond what you can bear. But when you are tempted, he will also provide a way out so that you can stand up under it.

1 CORINTHIANS 10:13

O kay, so every word that comes out of my mouth is sinful! I am a wretched excuse for a human being!" That is how I felt after examining the various kinds of wrong speech and seeing that I seem to have mastered every one of them.

Are you feeling somewhat hopeless at this point too? It's easy to think, "Well, then, what in the world *can* I say? Should I just take my vow of silence and go directly to a monastery right now, this instant? Do not pass GO. Do not collect $200."

God has provided us with healthy alternatives to unwholesome talk. He won't prevent us from being tempted, but He "will also provide a way out" (1 Corinthians 10:13). That means that He has given us ways to speak that do display godly character. Those alternatives are spelled out in His Word.

In order to make the right choices when faced with the temptation to use offensive talk, we must understand our options. While "wrong" words can be classified as careless, crafty, and corrupt; right words can be classified as controlled, compassionate, and credible.

MAKING THE CONTROLLED CHOICE

Controlled words are thoughtful words. The person speaking has taken the time to *think* before she opens her mouth. She has used that time to determine if the words she is planning to say are glorifying to God and helpful to the other person. Her words are careful and gentle. As Solomon noted:

> *The heart of the righteous weighs its answers,*
> *but the mouth of the wicked gushes evil.*
> Proverbs 15:28

Controlled words are good alternatives to *careless* words. Let's look at some of the types of careless words—such as anger, complaining, arguing, and foolish talk—and see what some more spiritually mature options are.

Alternatives to Anger

James 1:19 says, "Everyone should be quick to listen, slow to speak and slow to become angry." So the first step we can take when tempted to respond in anger is to *listen* and be *slow to speak.* Did your mother ever tell you to count to ten before talking to someone when you are mad? Mine did. She was actually restating Thomas Jefferson, who said, "If angry, count ten before you speak; if very angry, one hundred." Now that is control, and boy, is it hard to do!

When I find that my five-year-old son, Jimmy, has been willfully and repeatedly disobedient, sometimes I just start shouting at him. (If he thinks I am yelling, I assure him, "I am NOT yelling! This is how I always talk!") Sometimes Jimmy will attempt to appeal by saying, "But Mommy . . . ," to which my response is usually, "No 'But Mommy.' Just do as I say." Jimmy often points out that I am not listening. He is right. I am not listening at all. I am just responding in anger.

How could I respond instead? First I could shut my mouth, take my mother's advice, and count to ten. While counting, I could allow Jimmy to make his appeal and attentively listen. Then, given the cooling off period provided by listening, I could potentially correct or chastise him in a sensible manner. Quick to listen, slow to speak, slow to anger.

Now, the question is what would be a sensible response in this case? In Colossians 3, Paul urges believers to rid themselves of their old earthly ways and put on their new heavenly selves. Then he tells them,

> *Therefore, as God's chosen people, holy and dearly loved, clothe yourselves with compassion, kindness, humility, gentleness and patience.*
> Colossians 3:12

And in Ephesians 4 he says, "Be kind and compassionate to one another, forgiving each other, just as in Christ God forgave you" (v. 32).

In each of these passages, the qualities of compassion, kindness, humility, gentleness, patience, and forgiveness are the qualities that God has demonstrated toward us:

- His compassion toward us in our spiritual helplessness;
- His kindness toward us in reaching out to save us;
- His humility in leaving His glory in heaven to become human, to wash our feet as a model of service;
- His gentleness with us in our need;
- His patience with us in order to lead us to salvation;
- His forgiveness toward us so that we could have life and nearness to Him.

Scripture encourages us to live out the pattern of grace Christ has shown us. Maybe while I am being "slow to speak," I could be thinking, "How does my Father in heaven respond to me when I have been willfully disobedient, when I have been disrespectful to Him, or when I have ignored His words?" There is no doubt that He would be firm with me. There is also no doubt that He would also be loving and forgiving.

In my response to my son, I could listen to his appeal. If it was needed, I could deliver the appropriate level of discipline. Then, with kindness and compassion, I would explain why I considered his actions to be disobedient. I should never have to raise my voice if I am displaying compassion, patience, gentleness, and humility. Little Jimmy should never doubt my love for him or that I will forgive him. He should always see Christ in me.

How can I apply these elements of kindness, gentleness, compassion, and humility when I am angry with my husband? We have already determined that anger is not going to fix anything in the husband department. So how could I respond to him in order to express my feelings, yet not in anger?

Quick to listen, slow to anger. I could count to ten or excuse myself and go to another room until I am calm and can respond as God desires. I could gently say, "I need to go to the bedroom and cool off before I can talk about this further."

Once the emotion of anger has subsided, I could go back to my husband and say, "Honey, I love you. This is a really big issue for me. Can we talk about it now?"

Rage and wrath are varying levels of anger. When you are enraged by another or by circumstances and are tempted to use shrieks of rage or words of wrath, again, be quick to listen and slow to anger. When you do speak, use words of compassion, humility, patience, and gentleness. Take time to think of how Christ might respond in the same situation.

Choices Beyond Complaining

In chapter 2, we saw that we are not going to get our husbands (or anyone else) to do what we want by complaining and nagging.

A current television advertisement features children sitting at their supper table, looking at their plates of food saying, "Ew, what is that?" "I don't like that." "Do I *have* to eat that?" The catch phrase is, "Too much whine with dinner?" The solution is a particular brand of macaroni and cheese, I believe. Oh, if it were only that easy!

Jean, for example, seems to never be satisfied. Contentment is a stranger to her. No matter what it is—her house, her clothes, her curtains, her car—nothing is ever good enough. She complains all the time. In her case, saying nothing is likely the best option. Instead of whining and wearing out everyone around her, she could use the silence to contemplate all her blessings. Each of us has so much for which to be grateful, no matter how dire our circumstances. Beautiful children, health, a home, new nail polish, anything . . . find something to be grateful for.

When visiting with her friends, Jean could control her conversation by focusing on those things for which she is thankful. "I went to Albertson's this morning, and they just got in a shipment of shrimp from the coast! Can you believe it? We are having fresh shrimp for dinner tonight. What a blessing!"

When you find yourself in that crybaby-woe-is-me trap, close *your* trap. "Count your many blessings, name them one by one, and it will surprise you what the Lord hath done."[1] Stop. Count your blessings. Speak of the mercies of the Lord.

Antidotes to Arguing

I can argue with the best of them! I don't want to lose. In fact, I don't even enter an argument unless I know I can win. I want to negotiate or manipulate every argument to my advantage, to my desired outcome. Who doesn't?

But Proverbs 15:18 says, "A patient man calms a quarrel." Patience is another fruit our lives bear when we are centered in Christ. Rather than stoking the fires of an argument, we are called to calm a quarrel through a patient (not hotheaded) spirit. What exactly does that mean?

Sometimes it means walking away. Other times it means saying nothing at all. Still others, it means speaking words that will create peace. When faced with the opportunity to quarrel, honoring God needs to be more important than having our own way.

The Bible also commands us to return good for evil: "But I tell you who hear me: Love your enemies, do good to those who hate you, bless those who curse you, pray for those who mistreat you" (Luke 6:27–28; see also Romans 12:14, 17–18, 21). By doing this, we can stop the cycle of hostility and ill will.

If someone tries to pick a fight with you, don't give in. Return kindness to that person. Think, "What does this person need?" My husband submitted the following dialogue as a suggestion for wives when your husband comes home from work grumpy:

Him: (Whining, complaining, mean, angry, had-a-yucky-day kind of talk.) "Grump, grump, grump."
Her: "Honey, may I rub your feet?"

The computer technology business is very "dog-eat-dog." Very few women succeed in its environment. In my office, there was only one other woman. She didn't like that she had been there longer yet I had the one great account. Her frequent attempts to undermine my relationship with my customers or my reputation with my manager caused constant tension in the office. Because I have always believed "the nice guy always wins," instead of confronting her about her backstabbing, I was ridiculously kind to her. I prayed for her regularly. I advised her on her home decorating. I always asked her how her day was going, how her husband's business was going. I congratulated her on big deals she had won. I was genuinely kind most of the time, and, honestly, faked it if I absolutely had to. She didn't know quite what to do with me. My manager only saw me demonstrate grace and kindness, instead of participating in a catfight. Which one of us do you think had the advantage? When all else fails, just be nice.

Sometimes when my husband, Jimmy, and I get into an argument, it seems that I always have to have the last word. I just won't quit. I end up getting myself all worked up over what, in most cases, is really a very insignificant thing. Instead of continuing the argument, trying to put me in my place, defending himself, or simply telling me to shut up, Jimmy will put his arms around me and hold on for dear life, silently, until I calm down. Talk about calming a quarrel!

Preventives for Foolish Talk

I often catch myself saying something, only to immediately realize that it was a thoughtless, foolish thing to say. Do you do this too? How can we keep from embarrassing ourselves so?

Paul suggests in Ephesians 5:4 that we give thanks instead of talking thoughtlessly. What does that mean? I believe it means to speak of the mercies of the Lord. Talk about how grateful you are to God for the day, for the weather, for saving you. You could talk endlessly of what He has done for you. At a summer gathering of college friends one afternoon, I stood on a patio in the Oklahoma sunshine and visited with an old friend. It seemed that every sentence was about how God had blessed his life, how awesome God is, how gracious God is. I left thinking, "If only I had that kind of relationship with the Lord. Wow."

Not all foolish talk is purely thoughtless in the sense of being careless of another's feelings. What about when you are in a situation that catches you by surprise? You don't have a chance to think before you respond. For example: What if a man in whom you are completely uninterested romantically makes a play for you? How can you respond without making both you and this misguided fellow look foolish? You might respond, "You flatter me," and then quickly change the subject, giving the man a way out. We should be prepared for this event, because it inevitably happens to every woman at least once. (By the way, if the guy doesn't get the hint, see chapter 5 on speaking the truth in love. You may have to be brutally honest with him, but you can do it gracefully.)

What if you are at your husband's or boyfriend's company picnic and you don't know a soul and haven't a clue what to talk about? It is very easy to feel foolish in this situation if you are not prepared. Your folly then reflects poorly on your husband or boyfriend. One option in this scenario is to know his business. If he works for an investment firm, have a decent understanding of the market and of investing. If he works for a cement contractor, know about recent or upcoming projects.

I usually have a battery of questions prepared in my head when I enter a situation like this. At a wedding reception, for example: "How do you know Jana (the bride)?" "Oh, her roommate in college? How did you like Oklahoma State? What did you study? Marketing? So how did you use your education after college? Computer sales? What do you do now? Do you get to travel much in that position?" You can always make the other person feel at ease by being sincerely interested in her—all the while keeping yourself out of trouble. All it takes is a little forethought.

A controlled, godly woman is prepared for any situation. She has considered potential circumstances in which she might find herself. She has anticipated possible situations and surprises and is ready with a question or an answer that keeps her from talking foolishly. Her words make the listener feel important, and most significantly, her words glorify God as others see His gentleness in her.

MAKING THE COMPASSIONATE CHOICE

Compassionate words are caring, not crafty. They are edifying, not manipulating. They counter malicious or bitter words, slander, arrogance, or blasphemous, obscene words. The distinction is our motive. Our motivation for using crafty words is to manipulate, to denigrate, and to deprecate. Our motivation for compassionate words is to illuminate, to adulate, and to advocate. The exemplary woman ponders her motives before opening her mouth.

Better Than Bitterness and Malice

My motivation to speak maliciously has always been to make myself look smart, to be liked by my friends, and to make the other person feel stupid. I would make sarcastic, cutting remarks at another's expense because I wanted to be considered witty. I still catch myself spouting off these harsh words when I don't take time to think of the consequences.

Many of my friends have witnessed my not-so-Christlike wit so often that they will see it coming and literally duck for cover! Yes, I may get a chuckle from those around; the recipient of my dig might even chuckle and seemingly shake it off. However, the comment I made was intended to hurt the recipient and ultimately succeeds to some extent.

When tempted to speak maliciously, what other choices do we have? The first option is to say nothing at all. "If you can't say something nice, say nothing at all" (again, my mother's advice).

Scripture tells us to respond to others with kindness, compassion, gentleness, forgiveness, and forbearance—the same qualities Christ demonstrates to us. Many times kindness and compassion will dictate that we say nothing. Other times they will insist that we respond with an encouraging statement.

Sometimes the compassionate response will include criticism. That criticism must be offered gently and out of love. I have found that if criticism of any kind is required, it is always best delivered in private and after prayerful consideration. (Again, weigh your motives. Are they compassionate?)

Replacing malicious or bitter speech with compassion and respect extends even to telemarketers who interrupt our family dinners! Instead of yelling or slamming down the phone, why not say, "Excuse me. Do you have a no-call list?" (They are required by law to have one.) "Please put me on it. Thank you." Then, hang up the phone gently.

Many times reacting out of malice or bitterness is a result of another's harsh treatment of us or someone we love. In this case, we are called to exhibit forbearance. *Webster's* defines *forbearance* as "refraining from the enforcement of something (as a debt, right, or obligation) that is due; patience; leniency."[2] Forbearance makes us use our self-restraint. The world urges us to strike back with a verbal or physical beating. But God's way is different. In this case we need to walk away. If we must speak, we need to speak gently.

My husband and I frequently find ourselves in the company of a young man who seems to always be saying something hurtful to another person. This young man has a horrible reputation for arrogance and insolent behavior. When this happens, he deserves to be cut down to size. This is when I wish I were Julia Sugarbaker. Oh, I just want to rip him to shreds and point out to him that he is a dork! Once started, I probably wouldn't let up until he was in tears. (Like that is ever going to happen!) Forbearance means that even though he truly deserves severe treatment, I must refrain. As Paul counsels us:

> *Let your conversation be always full of grace.*
> Colossians 4:6

Stopping Slander

In Colossians, Paul admonishes us to speak with gentleness, compassion, and kindness (3:12). This means displaying excellence of character. Our choices as Christians here are to either say nothing or to say something edifying.

A miraculous change occurred in me a few months ago. After attending a meeting, I was visiting with a man and a woman who were present, and we were talking about a mutual friend who had received flowers from her husband every day that week because it was her birthday. We were going on about what a great guy this husband was! Well, the woman with whom I was talking said, "About half the time when my husband sends flowers, it is because he is in the doghouse!"

Imagine yourself in this situation. What would you have said at this point? I could have responded with, "Mine too!" and we all could have had a nice laugh at my husband's expense. Or, even worse, I could have said, "Oh, you are lucky. My husband is in the doghouse 95 percent of the time, and he *never* sends flowers, the bum!"

Thank the Lord that I didn't respond in either way. At this point, God's promise to refine my character with His Word became very real to me. My automatic response was, "Jimmy doesn't send flowers often, but honestly, I can't remember the last time he was in the doghouse!" I didn't even have to think about it. What a miracle. My friends' responses were, "Wow" and "Are you kidding?" They left there thinking not only more highly of my husband, but also thinking more highly of me! That is the grace of God at work in my life.

Shortly after a speaking engagement at which I shared this story, I heard from one of the precious women who had been in the audience that night, Teresa. She told me, "Not even a week after I heard you speak, Les and I were at a get-together with some other couples. The guys went out to the patio to talk about guy stuff—power tools or something. And that is when the girl talk began. When the other women began talking trash on their husbands, I had to say, 'I'm sorry, I can't talk like that about my husband.'" (I think she actually said, "Rhonda Webb says I can't talk about my husband that way." Whatever it takes!)

Either way, Teresa's response was perfect. Not only did she show respect for her husband, she also gave her friends cause to think that maybe they shouldn't be talking about their husbands that way either.

Obviously, not all slander is pointed toward our spouses. It could be about a girlfriend, a girlfriend's husband, an ex-husband, even an acquaintance. Whoever it is, if you are tempted, please consider Thumper's mother's advice in *Bambi:* "If you can't say something nice, say nothing at all."

I like rules and formulas. I probably have a little rule or formula for just about any situation in life. One of my rules used to be: You can say anything about another person as long as you follow it with, "Bless her heart." Here's an example: "Cynthia has gained so much weight . . . bless her heart." Well, this is a bad rule. I was wrong. When I encourage you to say something positive, I mean something 100 percent positive. Any statement that requires a "bless her heart" probably does not qualify.

Avoiding Arrogance and Boasting

The way to rid ourselves of arrogance and boasting is pretty straightforward. Put on humility, and use words that edify the listener—compassionate, gentle words.

How do we "put on" humility? We live Romans 12:10: "Honor one another above yourselves." To honor means to hold another in high esteem and in the highest regard.

If we catch ourselves speaking to someone else in a condescending way, we need to stop and apologize. A few rounds of apologizing for being a jerk will humble us if nothing else will!

Another way to ensure that we don't speak arrogantly is to always say "please" and "thank you." Address others with "ma'am" and "sir." By the way, "ma'am" and "sir" are not just reserved for our elders. What is wrong with answering a nineteen-year-old waitress with, "Yes, ma'am"? Not a thing. It should be expected in polite society.

I sat next to a gentleman (notice I used the word *gentleman*) at a Christmas dinner party last year. He finished every sentence with, "Yes, sir." When asked about his current construction project, he would answer, "It is a very exciting project, yes, sir." It was very charming—even though I am a "ma'am" and not a "sir."

If we catch ourselves bragging, the best thing to do is to

apologize for being so boastful. It is truly only because of God's grace that we could possibly have anything to be proud of.

James reminds us that our lives are really nothing but a mist that appears for a while and then vanishes (James 4:13–16). Really, if we think about it, what do we have to boast about? How smart we are? How beautiful we are? Why are we so smart or beautiful? Because God blessed us with brains and good looks. Does our intelligence or beauty compare with God's?

Margaret Thatcher, former British prime minister, said it best: "Being powerful is like being a lady. If you have to tell people you are, you aren't."

Finding a Way out of Filthy Language

Using vulgar language or cursing often becomes second nature to us. Breaking that habit can be almost as difficult as breaking the addiction to alcohol or tobacco.

James notes that words of praise to God and words of cursing should not come out of the same mouth (James 3:10). That makes me think that the best treatment for an addiction to using blasphemous, obscene language is to praise God instead. How does that work?

How about, when tempted to take God's name in vain, you pray, "Father, You are so awesome. You are greater and mightier than my tongue. Thanking You will help me speak only wholesome words." You could pray this out loud or silently from your heart. Either way, praising God in this way will stop you short of disobedience. It will save you from the sin of taking God's name in vain. And it will strengthen your character.

Another idea is to practice substituting acceptable words for profane words. My grandmother says phrases like, "Land o' Goshen!" "Goodness gracious" and "Land sake's alive." Sometimes, if the situation warrants, she combines all three statements: "Land-o-Goshen-goodness-gracious-land-sake's-alive." Another good grandma-ism is, "Great day in the morning." A friend of mine in grade school would say "Jumping Jupiter."

These kinds of phrases can be used instead of offensive exple-tives, and they show a lot more creativity.

Another option when ridding yourself of blasphemous talk is to speak gently. Gentleness of speech means you talk like a "lady," a "gentlewoman," instead of like a sailor. Gentleness, or gentle speech, is a natural benefit of having a Christ-centered heart. It is one of the fruits of the Spirit (Galatians 5:23). The more we pursue filling our hearts with God's Word and with His Holy Spirit, the more naturally we will bear the sweet fruit of gentleness. Again, Colossians 4:6 applies: "Let your conver-sation be always full of grace."

The result of this transformation in your speech and in your character will be an entirely new level of respect and honor from your peers.

Several years ago, during my career in the technology in-dustry, I was characterized by harsh, crass language. I was in a tough, stressful environment, and I thought I had to be rough and tough to succeed. Today, it is hard to believe that such lan-guage ever passed through my lips. Most of my friends would never believe me if I told them.

Recently, my husband and I hosted a dinner party with a Southern theme. The menu included cheese grits. If you are from the South, you already see a problem. A true Southerner would never put anything but a little butter in his or her grits. (And maybe a little salt and pepper.) During conversation at the din-ner table, I mentioned that my husband, being from Mississippi, considered cheese grits to be "bastardized." While I admit this may have not been the best choice of words, I mention it now because of the reaction at the table. All fourteen guests who had been involved in various conversations suddenly fell silent, and I saw fourteen faces staring at me, every jaw dropped. When one guest finally did speak, she said, "That wasn't Rhonda who said that? It couldn't have been Rhonda."

What a difference God has made in my life. I was once the one expected to use rough, off-color talk, and now no one will believe that those words can come out of my mouth, even if they hear it themselves.

Coarse joking and dirty stories were one of the primary reasons for my initial pursuit of God's will for our speech. I had witnessed Christians telling dirty jokes, repeatedly, even at Bible study. This really troubled me. It just didn't seem right to tell jokes that were offensive, especially during the time we had set aside to study God's Word. A dear friend of mine, being equally troubled, confronted an individual who was initiating this behavior during her small group Bible study. The man responded, "You are asking me to be a hypocrite. Why should I talk differently just because it is Bible study?" My friend wisely replied, "You shouldn't." A person professing to be a Christian should never use this kind of speech in any setting.

Will Smith, a.k.a. The Fresh Prince, started his astoundingly successful multimedia career as a rap artist. His first CD with DJ Jazzy Jeff contained many songs that were peppered with obscene language. Will's grandmother sent him a note after the release of this CD, which simply stated that educated, intelligent individuals did not need to use that kind of language to express themselves. Will's subsequent recordings are much more representative of his intelligence.[3]

Children seem to absorb bad language from school, cartoons, and movies. At our house, we censor closely what our son, Jimmy, is exposed to. However, even the most benign of cartoons or movies will include the word *stupid*. We have made a habit of all saying "beep" when we hear a word that we do not say at our house. It has helped little Jimmy to be aware of these words, recognizing them instead of just accepting them. Also, he will "beep" my husband and me every once in a while just to keep us accountable.

One more note on the use of off-color language. It is simply not feminine. It is not ladylike, appropriate, or becoming of a gentlewoman. I personally desire to be considered a strong woman by those around me, but not at the expense of my femininity. My mother raised me to be a lady. God created me to be a woman. Don't sacrifice that awesome gift in an effort to express your strength. A truly strong woman will choose another avenue of expression.

MAKING THE CREDIBLE CHOICE

Credible words reflect our integrity. They testify to the world that we belong to Christ because they are honest, true, respectable, and loving. Instead of using corrupt talk, we need to choose to deliberately articulate words that are commendable, blameless, virtuous, respectable, unimpeachable, and above reproach. Because these are the things we should be focused on, as Paul said:

> *Finally, brothers, whatever is true, whatever is noble, whatever is right, whatever is pure, whatever is lovely, whatever is admirable—if anything is excellent or praiseworthy—think about such things.*
> Philippians 4:8

When we follow this admonition from Paul to the Philippians, our words will reflect our thoughts. They will be words of excellence, of honor. They will be praiseworthy, pure, and admirable.

Leaving Lying Behind

Obviously, when a woman gives in to the temptation to lie, her words will not be credible. They are not honest and true. Our words will reflect our hearts and our level of integrity. We must choose if that reflection is positive or negative.

Once in a job interview I was asked, "Is it ever okay to lie?" I thought about it and my logical, well-thought-out answer was, "Yes, if lying was the only way to save a life." While I considered my answer quite impressive and noble, it really was the wrong answer. The Ten Commandments includes, "You shall not give false testimony" (Exodus 20:16). I don't know about you, but I get the impression that this means, "You shall not lie—*ever.*"

My thought process went like this: if someone was about to jump off a cliff to commit suicide, I might lie and tell him or her whatever he or she needed to hear to keep him or her from jumping. Now I see some flaws in my thinking. If my deceit did succeed in keeping that person from jumping, once he or she found out the truth, he or she might be right back at the edge. As Solomon wrote:

> *Truthful lips endure forever,*
> *but a lying tongue lasts only a moment.*
> Proverbs 12:19

Another flaw in my thinking was my lack of trusting God. I guess I thought, given the extreme situation, I should take things into my own hands. I was saying that God was not in control, and that disobeying God instead of trusting Him would fix things. God is so much bigger than my feeble efforts or my noble intentions. How in the world could I believe that my puny nobility could outperform the Almighty God?

All through the book of Proverbs (see NASB), we are encouraged to be truthful and not deceitful (see 3:3; 12:17; 14:22, 25; 16:6; 20:28; 23:23; 29:14). Truth is a natural outcome of filling our hearts with God's Word.

Have you ever watched a movie or a television show where the heroine is faced with a major decision of whether to lie or tell the truth? She is distressed over the possibility that the truth about her past might destroy her current relationship. (This is the stuff on which soap operas thrive.) As an observer, you know the whole situation. You know that telling the truth is ultimately in her best interest. As you sit in your seat, you are urging her, "Just tell the truth!" Does she? No, usually she chooses to lie, to cover up the truth, and the plot thickens. You, the observer, are thinking, "If you knew what I know, you would have told the truth. Lying is only going to make matters worse."

How much is that like our heavenly Father watching our lives? He is omniscient, all-knowing. When we are given the choice to be truthful or deceitful, don't you think our Father is urging us to be truthful? "If only you knew what I know . . . I will cause all things to work out for you. Just obey Me."

I encourage you, when tempted to be untruthful, do the right thing and trust God with the circumstances. Trust God to manage your relationships, your reputation, and your life. Put on truth.

Giving Gossip No Ground

"I just can't help it"—that's what many women say about gossip. Well, we *can* help it! First Corinthians 10:13 promises that we can:

> No temptation has seized you except what is common to man. And God is faithful; he will not let you be tempted beyond what you can bear. But when you are tempted, he will also provide a way out so that you can stand up under it.

Proverbs 11:13 contrasts the gossip with the trustworthy person: "A gossip betrays a confidence, but a trustworthy man keeps a secret." We can be trustworthy. Instead of spreading rumors or betraying a confidence, we can hold our tongues. Proverbs 12:23 says, "A prudent man keeps his knowledge to himself, but the heart of fools blurts out folly." Self-control is a fruit of the Spirit-filled life (Galatians 5:23).

When someone encourages you to participate in gossip, just say, "I am uncomfortable with this conversation." Or, "I don't think we should be talking about this." Or simply change the subject. You can do this without seeming self-righteous or judgmental if you practice.

I grew up in a small town, and gossip seems to be more rampant in small towns. I remember one lady in our church who was a perpetual gossip. If you wanted everyone in town to know your business, all you had to do was confide in her!

A few months ago, a dear friend of mine underwent some cosmetic surgery. She entrusted only one friend with this information. She did not want anyone to ever find out, but she really wanted someone to be praying for her. She came home from the hospital only to find out that nearly everyone she came in contact with knew every minute detail of her operation. She had confided in a gossip.

A gossip is not credible. No one trusts a gossip. When tempted to gossip, ask yourself, "Are these words credible? Are they honoring? Would I be saying this in front of the person of whom I am speaking?" A good rule of thumb is to never talk about another in his or her absence. Don't even think about using the "bless her heart" rule as an excuse either.

SUMMARY

Opening your mouth in wisdom begins with centering your heart in Christ. As you fill your heart with God's Word, you will be more apt to trust Him to take care of every situation, to provide you with options to temptation, and to cause all things to work out for your good.

Edifying, kind, godly speech will eventually become second nature to you. I promise it will not always seem so impossible.

You can never go wrong if you will seek, in every word, in every statement, in every response, to glorify your Father in heaven. As you do this, His character—truthful, kind, gentle, forgiving, compassionate, patient, and humble—will be vibrantly displayed in you.

≈ 4 ≈
Maybe Nobody
Heard That
Keeping Your Foot out of Your Mouth
. . . .

The heart of the righteous weighs its answers,

but the mouth of the wicked gushes evil.

PROVERBS 15:28

H ave you ever said something and immediately wanted to
kick yourself? "Oh, if only I could take those words back!"
Or your eyes dart about as you think hopefully, "Maybe nobody
heard that." The most dreadful feeling in the world comes over
you when you ask a woman, "When is your baby due?" and she
answers flatly, "I'm not pregnant." Couldn't you just crawl under a rock? When asked to reveal their most embarrassing moments, many people will tell that same story, almost verbatim.

I seem to have this uncanny ability to block embarrassing moments from my memory, so I can rarely come up with specific examples. But I do remember one time. I was at my grandmother's
house for a summer visit when I was about eight or nine. I was
sitting in the living room while she and a friend played Scrab-
ble, and I announced, "I'm bored." My grandmother, appalled

that I would say something so rude, exclaimed, "Rhonda Renee!" I responded with, "I meant, I am as stiff as a board," and tried to look really stiff.

I also remember the sinking feeling that comes when I have said something and wish immediately that no one heard it. I remember several sleepless nights with my stomach burning and my mind running over and over some ridiculous stream of words I had said that was just plain dumb. Solomon sure summed up my feelings:

> *You have been trapped by what you said,*
> *ensnared by the words of your mouth.*
> Proverbs 6:2

Have you ever felt trapped or ensnared by something you said? Why is it that so often our words get us into trouble, that we wish we could catch them and stuff them back down our throats? I believe it is primarily because we don't truly understand the power of words. It is in this naïveté that we allow rash, careless words to fly off our tongues like darts. In order to keep our feet on the floor and out of our mouths, we must first pay heed to the power of our words, then specifically identify the careless, rash words that will humiliate us, and finally learn to think before we speak.

THE POWER OF WORDS

Templeton kept out of sight. In the tall grass behind the cattle barn he found a folded newspaper. Inside it were leftovers from somebody's lunch: a deviled ham sandwich, a piece of Swiss cheese, part of a hard-boiled egg, and the core of a wormy apple. The rat crawled in and ate everything. Then he tore a word out of the paper, rolled it up and started back to Wilbur's pen.

Charlotte had her web almost finished when Templeton returned, carrying the newspaper clipping. She had left a space in the middle of the web. At this hour, no people were around the pigpen, so the rat and the spider and the pig were by themselves.

"I hope you brought a good one," Charlotte said. "It is the last word I shall ever write."

"Here," said Templeton, unrolling the paper.

"What does it say?" asked Charlotte. "You'll have to read it for me."

"It says 'Humble,'" replied the rat.

"'Humble'?" said Charlotte. "'Humble' has two meanings. It means 'not proud' and it means 'near the ground.' That's Wilbur all over. He's not proud and he's near the ground."[1]

In *Charlotte's Web,* by E. B. White, Charlotte used words to save the life of her best friend. "Some Pig." "Terrific." "Radiant." "Humble." Using these five simple words, she succeeded. Wilbur the pig was not only saved, but he lived a life of luxurious buttermilk baths, fresh straw, and warm feed. What a wonderful illustration of the power of words.

As I was growing up, my dad told me over and over and over, "Rhonda Renee, you can do anything you set your mind to." "You are smart." "You can do this." As far back as I can remember, he was soldering those phrases into my thinking.

When I left college after my sophomore year and went to work as a receptionist, I made a profound and monumental decision that I would not finish college. Instead, I would pursue a career as a receptionist and possibly advance to be a secretary some day. Daddy was adamant that this plan was not acceptable. I could do anything I set my mind to . . . I could be president of the United States if I set my mind to it. I was thwarting my potential. "Rhonda Renee . . ." Shortly thereafter I enrolled in college again and three years later, graduated.

The year I graduated, statistics said that the average college graduate would earn a certain salary in his or her first year out of college. Well, by this time my dad's urgings had succeeded to some degree, and I thought, "Since I am *above* average, I should earn more than the average college graduate." Everyone around me, except my parents, said it was not possible, especially in Oklahoma. Maybe in New York or L.A., but new graduates just don't earn that much in Tulsa, Oklahoma. Well, I did it. And subsequently, my professional career exceeded even my expectations. (Although my achievements didn't seem to surprise my parents at all!)

I earnestly believe that my dad saying, "Rhonda Renee, you can do anything you set your mind to," was the foundation for any and every success I have experienced. Words are powerful.

> *"I tell you the truth, if anyone **says** to this mountain, 'Go, throw your-self into the sea,' and does not doubt in his heart but believes that what he says will happen, it will be done for him."*
>
> Mark 11:23 (emphasis added)

Words are powerful.

> *Whoever would love life and see good days must* **keep his tongue** *from evil and his lips from deceitful speech.*
>
> 1 Peter 3:10 (emphasis added)

Words are powerful.

> *When we put bits into the mouths of horses to make them obey us, we can turn the whole animal. Or take ships as an example. Although they are so large and are driven by strong winds, they are steered by a very small rudder wherever the pilot wants to go. Likewise the tongue is a small part of the body, but it makes great boasts. Consider what a great forest is set on fire by a small spark.* **The tongue also is a fire,** *a world of evil among the parts of the body. It corrupts the whole person, sets the whole course of his life on fire, and is itself set on fire by hell.*
>
> *All kinds of animals, birds, reptiles and creatures of the sea are be-ing tamed and have been tamed by man, but no man can tame the tongue. It is a restless evil, full of deadly poison.*
>
> James 3:3–8 (emphasis added)

Words are powerful.

Are you convinced yet? Our words can move mountains in our lives. Just *say* it. If you want to see good days and enjoy life, what is the one thing you have to do? Watch your tongue! Your tongue is such a small thing, but, oh, the power. It corrupts the whole person. It doesn't matter if you have scrubbed every millimeter of your body with lye soap, if you have cleansed your colon, or laundered your liver with herbs and cranberry juice. If your words are defiled, your very character is defiled.

Words are powerful. Please handle with care.

CARELESS AND RASH WORDS

If words are that powerful, how can we just fling them here and there without concern? Have you ever seen how a four- or five-year-old flower girl in a wedding tosses rose petals from a basket? She is looking up or looking down or crying from fear, and all the petals seem to end up in a pile instead of ideally arranged down either side of the bride's path. This is how we are with words. How can we be so careless? Speaking rashly is no less negligent than tossing a lit match out the car window while on a scenic tour of Yosemite National Forest.

Look again at James' words:

> *And the tongue is a flame of fire. It is full of wickedness that can ruin your whole life. It can turn the entire course of your life into a blazing flame of destruction, for it is set on fire by hell itself.*
>
> James 3:6 (NLT)

Examples from Life

For example, when her husband's inattentiveness hurts Jeannie, she lashes out at him with harsh words before thinking —"The house is not big enough" . . . "If you made more money, we could live in a nicer house" . . . "If you were more responsible, we could join the country club" . . . "All of our friends have nicer cars." Jeannie goes on and on without thinking of the consequences. Then she is surprised when, after twelve years of marriage, Bert wants a divorce. Well, of course he does. She has made him feel worthless for twelve years. Someone else out there speaks kindly to him and values him. Jeannie can't imagine why Bert would want to leave. She can't even remember saying all those cruel things. She was just spouting off. They didn't mean anything.

But they did.

These are careless, rash words. Jeannie doesn't want a divorce, but she never stopped to think of the power of her words. Each little spark ignited by her words had the power to incinerate her marriage.

Here's another example. Stan is a hardworking man. He can't help but bring the stresses of his work home with him at night. But when things at home don't go exactly as he plans, he erupts with an angry, drilling tirade peppered with coarse, accusing words. Six years of this and he is amazed that Jill has found another man who tells her she is beautiful and engaging, who appreciates her and tells her so.

Stan's words are rash and careless. They, like Jeannie's words, have the power to destroy a marriage.

Yet another illustration is Sarah. Sarah loves to talk. Gab, gab, gab. She could make conversation with anyone. "Oh, you don't say. My good friend Penny is a horrible cook too! Her poor husband has to do all the cooking at their house. Boy, that's the life. You know, I don't know what she does with her time. She must just sit around eating bonbons by the pool all day. Now, Cindy—oh, you know Cindy, don't you? Well, she loves to cook, but Tom, you know her husband, Tom. He never comes home from work before ten o'clock so she never gets to cook. I cook some, but Bob is so finicky. He will only eat hamburger meat. So, I am stuck making Hamburger Helper every night. You know there is a new flavor . . ."

Sarah goes on and on. She has carelessly put down at least

three people in a matter of seconds. Suddenly she realizes that none of her "good friends" are calling her anymore. No one will confide in her or even talk to her anymore. She has no idea why.

Sarah's words are careless. She doesn't consider how many people she has hurt deeply with her words. Her words have the power to ruin her reputation, uproot her integrity, and annihilate her relationships. As Solomon cautions:

> *Reckless words pierce like a sword,*
> *but the tongue of the wise brings healing.*
> Proverbs 12:18

One more example. Sharon is quite a talker too. She likes to hear the sound of her own voice. She will tell just about anyone who will listen all about her and Jack's latest sexual escapades in detail or all about their most recent vacation, play-by-play. Who needs pictures? She could talk for hours about her son's latest run-in with "that crazy teacher, Mrs. Jones." She doesn't understand why people seem to be avoiding her or why they are always wandering off right when she is in the middle of a great story.

Sharon's words are careless. They are powerful enough to make others avoid her like the plague. They are powerful enough to stealthily take away her joy. She has no idea what is happening.

God's Word describes these people in Ecclesiastes:

> *Words from a wise man's mouth are gracious,*
> *but a fool is consumed by his own lips.*
> *At the beginning his words are folly;*
> *at the end they are wicked madness—*
> *and the fool multiplies words.*
> *No one knows what is coming—*
> *who can tell him what will happen after him?*
> Ecclesiastes 10:12–14

Do you know anyone who just seems to drone on and on about nothing? Someone who seems to like to hear herself talk as you are frantically searching for some reason to get away? How about someone who is constantly interrupting others or finishing their sentences? These are examples of how a fool's words consume her and how a fool multiplies words. Could that fool be you?

Examples from Scripture

In Judges 11, Jephthah made a careless vow to the Lord (vv. 30–32). He vowed that if God would deliver the Ammonites into his hands, whatever first came out of his house when he arrived home would be sacrificed as a burnt offering. Well, God did deliver the Ammonites, and Jephthah returned home triumphant. As he was approaching his house, however, the first thing he saw was his daughter, his only child, who ran out to greet him. Because he made a promise to the Lord, he had to sacrifice his only child.

The gospel of Mark gives the account of Herod hosting an exotic dinner party. To supplement the lavish banquet, the daughter of Herodias danced for the guests. Herod was so pleased with her performance that he promised her anything up to half of his kingdom. She asked for the head of John the Baptist on a platter! Since he made the oath in front of all his dinner guests, he felt obligated to grant her request (6:14–29). Careless, rash words.

Humans have been getting themselves into trouble with their reckless tongues for thousands of years. Why don't we ever learn?

THINK BEFORE YOU SPEAK

Donald Rumsfeld, the U.S. secretary of defense, is in charge of planning and executing America's war against terrorism. On CBS's *60 Minutes II*, David Martin interviewed him in November 2001, and he says of Rumsfeld:

He often takes a long pause before answering reporters' questions. *"I'm old-fashioned. I like to engage my brain before my mouth,"* he jokingly told reporters at one press conference.

Some say he has put the thrill back in the press conference because nobody knows what he will say in response.[2] (emphasis added)

When asked a question by one of the press corps, Rumsfeld will just freeze in silence for what seems like minutes on end before he answers. His style in press briefings earned him the "ultimate cultural cachet"—the opening skit on *Saturday Night Live.* His pregnant pauses were the stars of the parody!

But Solomon praises the wisdom of the pause:

> *He who guards his lips guards his life,*
> *but he who speaks rashly will come to ruin.*
> Proverbs 13:3

We need to engage our minds before we engage our mouths. How can we do that? I believe the first and most important step to thinking before speaking is to simply slow down:

> *Everyone should be quick to listen,* **slow to speak**
> *and slow to become angry.*
> James 1:19 (emphasis added)

If we just slow down enough to think, we could save ourselves a lot of humiliation. What is so all-fired important that we can't wait two seconds before we blurt it out? I have found that if I feel an urgency to speak—like I just have to squeeze some really "important" statement into a running conversation—that is a big red flag. It says, "Slow Down."

At some level, rushing our words into existence is arrogance. We must be thinking subconsciously that our words are so important that they need to be spoken first or fastest. We need to beat everyone else to the punch. What is up with that?

Once you have slowed the pace and taken a breath, what are

you supposed to think about your preexistent words? I believe the most important thought to apply is, "Is what I am about to say going to glorify the Father?" Peter, who in his early years often opened his mouth only to switch feet, learned this:

If anyone speaks, he should do it as one speaking the very words of God.
1 Peter 4:11

My friend Julie has a technique she calls "fast-forward thinking." This is when you think, "If I say this, what will happen afterward? Will I be glad I said it? Will I wish I could take it back?"

I fail at this so many times. I have learned the hard way to think before I speak. I have been shamed and disgraced too many times by insipid, vapid, tedious, senseless statements that seem to stream from my mouth. Yet even so, when I question whether my words will glorify God, many times I determine they will not, and I still choose to speak them. I choose to communicate in ways that conflict with my proclamation of Christianity.

So what's a girl to do? Slow down, think, then what? How about buck up and show a little self-control! Solomon observed that "a man of knowledge uses words with restraint" (Proverbs 17:27). As we edge ever closer to that desired relationship with the Father by filling our hearts with His Word and living out the urgings of the Holy Spirit, that discipline and that discretion will become more and more a natural function. It, too, is a fruit of the Spirit-filled life.

Deliberating and using discretion before speaking is a discipline. Once we recognize the power of words, we must cultivate the habit of (1) slowing down, (2) thinking "Will my words glorify God?", and (3) suppressing whatever speech is not glorifying to God.

Like King David, we can pray each day:

Set a guard over my mouth, O LORD;
keep watch over the door of my lips.
Psalm 141:3

5

Well, It's the Truth!

Speaking the Truth in Love

· · · · · · · · · · · · · · ·

Instead, speaking the truth in love, we will in all things grow up into him who is the Head, that is, Christ.

EPHESIANS 4:15

Men occasionally stumble on the truth, but most of them pick themselves up and hurry off as if nothing had happened.

SIR WINSTON CHURCHILL

E verything is relative. There is no absolute truth."

"Truth for you may not be truth for someone else."

Popular secular recording artist, Alanis Morissette says of her music, "I know that what I am singing about is the truth, *my* truth."[1]

In the twenty-first century, we are bombarded with this kind of mumbo jumbo. Television, movies, and popular music all enforce the belief that truth is relative, not absolute. Culture tells us that truth is, in essence, more a matter of convenience than a matter of foundation.

If you are sixteen but want to see an R-rated movie, what do you do? You just lie. Goodness, you could even manufacture a fake ID card. It's convenient. Nobody gets hurt, and nobody gets caught.

Women shop and spend extravagantly but tell their husbands that the $200 dress was really on sale for $50. Nobody gets hurt. It's just easier for everybody this way.

This is what we tell ourselves. We are, in fact, not only lying to others—we are lying to ourselves.

How in the world did we get to this point of disillusionment? Although to today's Christian it seems our society has taken twisting or questioning truth to the extreme, this duplicity is really nothing new.

When interrogating Jesus, Pilate cynically asked Him, "What is truth?" (John 18:38). He was in essence saying, "Truth is relative. What is truth, anyway?" When we discount or question the basis of truth in this way, we have undermined the basis of justice, and moral right and wrong. Satan has been cunningly obscuring absolute truth since the beginning of time. And we have been falling for it! Look at Eve, for goodness' sake.

WHAT IS TRUTH?

As Christian women, it is fundamental that we accept nothing less than truth. It is essential that we speak nothing in addition to truth. As Jesus teaches us:

"Simply let your 'Yes' be 'Yes,' and your 'No,' 'No'; anything beyond this comes from the evil one."
                                        Matthew 5:37

Truth is foundational to our faith:

"I am the way and the truth and the life. No one comes to the Father except through me."
                                        John 14:6

As I searched worldly sources like literature and the dictionary to help me define truth, I was not only terribly disappointed but also astounded.

Webster's defines *truth* as "sincerity in action, character, and utterance; the state of being the case: fact; the body of real things, events, and facts: actuality; a transcendent fundamental or spiritual reality; fidelity to an original or to a standard."[2] Even if I give Mr. Webster the benefit of the doubt and say the "original" is God's Word, there is still room for truth to be interpreted by the world's "standard." Reading this, I thought, "No wonder our society thinks truth is relative."

Deep thinkers seem to be somewhat ambiguous about truth as well:

Whatever satisfies the soul is truth.

—WALT WHITMAN

It is always the best policy to speak the truth, unless of course you are an exceptionally good liar.

—JEROME K. JEROME

In the province of the mind, what one believes to be true either is true or becomes true.

—JOHN LILLY

I then went to *Strong's Universal Subject Guide to the Bible.* It defines *truth* as "that which agrees with final reality."[3] Well, gosh. Does that mean that we will never really know truth until the end of time, when we see what lines up with the final reality? That definition didn't seem to help me much either. I was still dissatisfied.

As I frantically looked through book after book, I was amazed that I couldn't find any concrete definition for such a solid and substantial word. I resolved to go to the Source: the Bible. I looked at all the Old Testament Hebrew words for truth. I found about six different words that are interpreted as *truth* in Hebrew. Ah, finally, something I could sink my teeth into. *Truth* in the Old Testament meant "certainty, stability,"[4] "to render firm, permanent,"[5] "firmness, security, faithfulness,"[6] "balanced,"[7] "established,"[8] and "something fixed."[9] What a difference!

Now that I had a more sound definition for truth, I looked up in today's dictionary some of the words that were synonymous with truth in Hebrew. (Now, I am trying to trick Webster!) *Stability* is "the strength to stand or endure: firmness; the property of a body that causes it when disturbed from a condition of equilibrium or steady motion to develop forces or moments that restore the original condition."[10]

Permanent means "continuing or enduring without fundamental or marked change."[11]

Firm is "securely or solidly fixed in place; not weak or uncertain; not subject to change or revision; not easily moved or disturbed: steadfast."[12]

At this point in my search, I was feeling a little better. At least I had a more definitive perception of what the word *truth* really means. It is *not* relative. It is *not* different for different people. It is permanent, fixed, established, certain, and stable. It has not, nor will it ever, change. There is only One who has never, nor will ever, change. He is the living God, I AM. He *is* truth. There is only one "standard" that has not, nor will ever, change. That is God's Word. His words *are* truth.

So now that we know what truth is, we can move on to the next step. Actually speaking the truth. Sometimes it is really painful or awkward to be truthful. What if telling the truth will hurt someone's feelings? What if it will most likely make another uncomfortable or even angry? It has been said, "The truth hurts." So how do we deal with that? Speaking the truth in love, we trust God to handle the rest.

WHAT DOES IT MEAN
TO SPEAK THE TRUTH IN LOVE?

One afternoon a few years ago, about a week after my Uncle Andy died, I spoke to my mother on the phone. She was struggling with the loss of her oldest brother. Her next oldest brother's wife was fighting breast cancer, and Mama was dealing with horrible headaches coupled with severe back and neck pain. It was a very difficult time for her, obviously.

As we were talking, Mama said something like, "I'm falling apart, Andy is gone, and Doris is not doing any good at all." (That is Oklahoma-talk for "Doris is really sick.") "Could things get any worse?"

I replied with my pompous, Pollyanna attitude, "Of course things could get worse! Good grief, Mom, how negative can you be?"

Well, I spoke the truth. But, oh my! Certainly not in a very loving way.

My mom was hurting. She needed some compassion. The same truth spoken in an attitude of love might have sounded like, "Mama, I am sorry things are so rough right now. I love you. It comforts me to know that God is in control." I could have offered to pray with her, thanking God that Uncle Andy was with Him in heaven, that the Lord is the God who heals, that He is sovereign and has a plan for our lives—to give us a future and a hope. I could have, but I didn't.

Do you see the difference? The truth was that things could have been much worse. That our hope is in the Lord. It was my choice to either communicate that truth indignantly or to communicate that truth in a loving way. I made the wrong choice.

Ephesians 4:15 says as believers we should be "speaking the truth in love." The primary way I reveal my love for God is by loving others:

Jesus replied: "'Love the Lord your God with all your heart and with all your soul and with all your mind.' This is the first and greatest commandment. And the second is like it: 'Love your neighbor as yourself.'"
Matthew 22:37–39

"A new command I give you: Love one another. As I have loved you, so you must love one another. By this all men will know that you are my disciples, if you love one another."
John 13:34–35

Dear friends, let us love one another, for love comes from God. Everyone who loves has been born of God and knows God. Whoever does not love does not know God, because God is love.
1 John 4:7–8

God's Word consistently connects truth with loving God and loving others:

"If you love me, you will obey what I command."
John 14:15

Therefore each of you must put off falsehood and speak truthfully to his neighbor, for we are all members of one body.
Ephesians 4:25

"These are the things you are to do: Speak the truth to each other."
Zechariah 8:16

Now that you have purified yourselves by obeying the truth so that you have sincere love for your brothers, love one another deeply, from the heart.
1 Peter 1:22

Truth often requires us to challenge a brother or sister in Christ with the reality that his or her behavior is ungodly. I think I would just rather ignore the situation, but God's Word tells me otherwise:

"And if your brother sins, go and reprove him in private; if he listens to you, you have won your brother."
Matthew 18:15 (NASB [1977])

What I find so interesting about all this is that we, as Christians in the twenty-first century, seem to be doing everything but what we are called to do. Either we are avoiding speaking truth out of fear of offending or hurting someone, or we are speaking the truth so roughly that we are not showing love at all but cold, hard piety instead. God's way is the best way—tenderly speaking God's truth to one another.

The apostle Paul was required to relate some difficult truths to the people in the church of Thessalonica. Shortly after he had established the church there, Paul found that the people were operating under some misconceptions about the second coming of Christ, and some had become irresponsible in other ways as well. Paul had to tell them that they were wrong. He could have said, "What, are you people nuts? What are you thinking? Didn't you listen to a word I said?" But he didn't. The elements of Paul's first letter to the Thessalonians illustrate the meaning of "speaking the truth in love":

- *Affirmation.* Paul affirms the Thessalonians' witness for Christ in chapter 1, telling them that he thanks God for their faithful, loving work and hopeful endurance of suffering.

- *Relationship.* In chapter 2, Paul reviews his relationship to the people, reminding them that he treated them with dignity. He cared for them as a mother cares for her little children and guided them like a father. He shared his life with them. In chapter 3, he tells these believers who are so precious to him that he longed to be with them and to know how they were doing. He even sent Timothy on ahead of him to find out.

- *Warning and reproof.* In chapter 4, Paul had the difficult task of pointing out to these new believers that they needed to steer clear of sexual impurity. Also, some of them had started living a life of idleness and were depending on others for handouts. They were not being responsible. Paul had to reprove them for this behavior. He then recounts for them the specifics about the coming of the Lord in order to clear up any confusion they may have had.

- *Encouragement.* Paul ends his letter with encouragement in chapter 5. He tells them how they can find hope in the truth he has told them and asks them to encourage one another.

First Thessalonians, in a nutshell, is Paul speaking the truth in love. It is:

Truth (reproof and/or warning) communicated with *affirmation* and *encouragement* in the context of a historical *relationship* of caring and commitment.

Relationship is key here. If you express truth to someone with whom your historical relationship is one of disrespect, insolence, or hatred, how would you expect them to believe you, much less even want to speak to you? Without the relationship, there is no basis, no foundation, for people to accept what you have to tell them. You've heard, "Talk is cheap." Well, that statement fits here. How could you possibly expect someone to embrace anything you have to say if there is no relationship?

For example, Linda's divorce was not final. Her husband, Ken, just didn't seem to care about her or show affection to her anymore. Her friend John, however, was attractive and attentive. He made her feel special. Although she wasn't yet divorced, what started as a friendship with John grew into a very intimate relationship. They were not only sleeping together, but they were going to church together as well.

Christy was a godly woman. She was only an acquaintance of Linda's but was very upset by Linda's sin. Christy went to Linda in private and told her that her relationship with John was not right; it was sin. Even though Linda and John were seeking spiritual growth together, their relationship would never be acceptable to God. It had to end.

Christy spoke the truth. She had pure motives. But she had no relationship with Linda that would encourage Linda to accept this difficult truth from her. Christy could tell Linda how much she loved her until she was blue in the face, but there was no history of devotion or mutual esteem. Needless to say, Linda didn't take Christy's interference very well. Her relationship with John did not end. This occurred years ago, and there is still bitterness between Christy and Linda.

Can you see the marked distinction between just communicating truth and speaking the truth in love?

I am often frustrated when I read a book that defines a difficult concept but doesn't tell me *how* to apply the principles practically. So, now that we have an understanding of what it means to speak the truth in love, how do we actually do it?

HOW TO SPEAK THE TRUTH IN LOVE

Scripture offers us a perfect guide for communicating truth in a spirit of love in John 4, the account of the Samaritan woman's encounter with Jesus. One caveat: This example goes against the previous definition, in that Jesus had never met this woman before this encounter. I still believe that the relationship factor is the key to speaking the truth in love for us. However, Jesus, being God, did not have the relational limitations that we do. He knew everything about her. He knew her when she was in her mother's womb (Psalm 139). He *is* perfect love personified. With that in mind, here is the story of Jesus and the woman of Samaria.

Now he had to go through Samaria. So he came to a town in Samaria called Sychar, near the plot of ground Jacob had given to his son Joseph. Jacob's well was there, and Jesus, tired as he was from the journey, sat down by the well. It was about the sixth hour [noon].

When a Samaritan woman came to draw water, Jesus said to her, "Will you give me a drink?" (His disciples had gone into the town to buy food.)

The Samaritan woman said to him, "You are a Jew and I am a Samaritan woman. How can you ask me for a drink?" (For Jews do not associate with Samaritans.)

Jesus answered her, "If you knew the gift of God and who it is that asks you for a drink, you would have asked him and he would have given you living water."

"Sir," the woman said, "you have nothing to draw with and the well is deep. Where can you get this living water? Are you greater than our father Jacob, who gave us the well and drank from it himself, as did also his sons and his flocks and herds?"

Jesus answered, "Everyone who drinks this water will be thirsty again, but whoever drinks the water I give him will never thirst. Indeed, the water I give him will become in him a spring of water welling up to eternal life."

The woman said to him, "Sir, give me this water so that I won't get thirsty and have to keep coming here to draw water."

He told her, "Go, call your husband and come back."

"I have no husband," she replied.

Jesus said to her, "You are right when you say you have no husband. The fact is, you have had five husbands, and the man you now have is not your husband. What you have just said is quite true."

"Sir," the woman said, "I can see that you are a prophet. Our fathers worshiped on this mountain, but you Jews claim that the place where we must worship is in Jerusalem."

Jesus declared, "Believe me, woman, a time is coming when you will worship the Father neither on this mountain nor in Jerusalem. You Samaritans worship what you do not know; we worship what we do know, for salvation is from the Jews. Yet a time is coming and has now come when the true worshipers will worship the Father in spirit and truth, for they are the kind of worshipers the Father seeks. God is spirit, and his worshipers must worship in spirit and in truth."

The woman said, "I know that Messiah" (called Christ) "is coming. When he comes, he will explain everything to us."

Then Jesus declared, "I who speak to you am he."

John 4:4–26

This passage provides us with six steps to follow when speaking the truth to another:

1. Authenticate your motive.
2. Approach in private.
3. Assert your love.
4. Afford an opportunity to confess.
5. Articulate only the facts.
6. Affirm and encourage.

Authenticate Your Motive

Jesus had to go through Samaria on His way from Judea to Galilee. Actually, He didn't *have* to. Most Jews would have gone out of their way to avoid Samaria. He went through Samaria because it was the shortest way to Galilee, which is where the Father wanted Him to go. Being all-knowing, He knew that the Samaritan woman would be at the well. However, His primary motive was to obey God. His secondary motive was to show that true worship comes from your heart and is not dependent on your heritage, your social position, or your worthiness.

His motive was not to express moral or religious prejudices. He also had no intention of addressing the Jewish travel policies.

Sometimes we think that we *must* tell some others the truth. But really, we want to hurt them or make them feel ashamed. By God, we are going to show them their wicked ways! Those heathens! Jesus' motive, however, was to glorify the Father. Ours should be as well.

Approach in Private

Jesus spoke with the Samaritan woman in private, after the disciples had gone into town. Now, He wasn't confronting her but simply speaking with her. His example, however, can instruct us when we need to confront someone. As our Lord said in Matthew's gospel, we are to reprove our brother or sister in private:

*"If your brother sins against you, go and show him his fault,
just between the two of you."*

Matthew 18:15

I believe it is important to point out that a married woman
should never go to a man alone in this situation. If you are required to reprove a brother in Christ, take your husband with
you. The best solution would be for your husband to go to that
man with a reproof. As Christian women, we should never give
the appearance or the opportunity for impropriety.

Assert Your Love

The woman at the well was not only Samaritan but poor as
well. She was a social outcast. How do we know this about her?
A woman of any wealth at all would not draw her own water.
A woman who was socially accepted would come to the well in
the cool of the morning, not in the heat of the day. She was most
likely trying to avoid the people from her town.

Due to cultural and historical issues, Jews abhorred Samaritans.
A Jew would not speak to a Samaritan man, much less a woman.
Just the fact that Jesus spoke to her is huge. Not even people of
her own city spoke to her. At first she thought He must think her a
loose woman. She was suspicious of this Jew but soon realized that
Jesus was sincere. By speaking to her, Jesus showed that He had
regard for her. He didn't consider her to be the scum of the earth.

Afford an Opportunity to Confess

You don't need to approach someone and preach to her about
her sin if she already knows it is sin. Jesus asked the woman to
go and get her husband. He knew she did not have one. This gave
her a chance to come clean with him.

Articulate Only the Facts

Give God's view, not your opinion. In John 4, Jesus said, "You
are right when you say you have no husband. The fact is, you

have had five husbands, and the man you now have is not your husband. What you have just said is quite true" (vv. 17–18).

He could have said, "You're right, you don't have a husband. What, do you just marry every man who says hello to you? Good grief, woman, you have had five husbands, and you are shacking up with another man even now! Your sin is disgusting." He could have, but He didn't.

Regarding my earlier story of Linda and Christy, if Christy had had the relationship with Linda to support her candor, she could have said, "God hates divorce (Malachi 2:16). You are still married to Ken, and you are already sleeping with a man who is not your husband." What more needs to be said? No opinion need be offered here.

Many times we forget that while God may choose to use us to point out the truth, it is the Holy Spirit's job to stir conviction in another's heart. Jimmy and I have personally experienced this and have seen others dealing with it in our circle of friends. It seems there is a profusion of marriages breaking up around us in recent years. We have stepped in to provide counsel and encouragement for many of these couples. While we have offered godly advice, provided practical ways of communicating, and rendered reproof when required, sometimes the troubled spouses still proceed with divorce. We are so discouraged and feel like we have failed when this happens. We have even considered locking up the two in a room until they work it out! Still, the bottom line is that *we* cannot make them stay married. We can only obey God in discouraging their actions and encouraging them to work things out. We also must be obedient to love them, even when they don't do what we believe to be right. Then we have to trust God with the rest. We have to remember that He is sovereign.

Affirm and Encourage

Jesus encouraged the woman. He told her she could worship God from her heart. It didn't matter if she was a Jew or a Samaritan; her praise was just as acceptable to God as that of a Jew.

SUMMARY

As we walk through our lives here in the twenty-first century, we must never forget that truth is *not* relative. It is absolute, permanent, fixed. It has never changed or moved throughout time, nor will it ever.

As believers in Jesus Christ, we are commanded to speak truth. It is not enough to simply blurt out true statements. We are called to communicate truth in a spirit of love. Speaking the truth in love is: *"Truth (warning or reproof) communicated with affirmation and encouragement in the context of a historical relationship characterized by love and devotion."*

Anyone can choose to verbalize true statements. The Christ-like woman, however, is typified by words of truth that affirm, encourage, and manifest love to the listener. These words bring glory to our Father.

I have no greater joy than to hear that my children
are walking in the truth.

3 John 4

6
I *Had* to
Say Something!
A Time for Silence

. . . .

There is a time for everything,
and a season for every activity under heaven: . . .
a time to be silent and a time to speak.

ECCLESIASTES 3:1, 7

Marguerite was a delightful child, although she had had more than her share of difficulties. When she was three, her parents divorced and she went to live with her grandmother. But when she was seven, it seemed her mother had her life in order, so little Marguerite and her brother excitedly went back to live with her. That year, this charming little girl was raped by her mother's boyfriend. Days later she finally told her brother what had happened, and the man was arrested and subsequently was found dead, having been kicked to death. Thinking her words had killed him, Marguerite stopped talking.

After this horrendous experience, Marguerite went back to live with her grandmother, where she remained silent for nearly six years.

This story is true. Marguerite grew up to be the internationally acclaimed speaker, author, poet, playwright, actress, producer, director, and scholar Maya Angelou. She speaks six languages fluently. She is the author of ten best-selling books. She wrote and delivered the poem "On the Pulse of the Morning" for the inauguration of President Clinton. She was nominated for a Pulitzer Prize for her poem "Just Give Me a Cool Drink of Water 'Fore I Die." She received a Grammy award for "Best Spoken Word or Non-musical Album" for *Phenomenal Women* in 1995. She has been nominated for Tony Awards, Emmy Awards, and numerous other literary distinctions and honorary degrees as well. Her awards and accomplishments are too abundant to list.

She speaks with incomparable confidence, authority, and a mesmerizing cadence. It has been said of her skill as a public speaker, "I felt that this woman could have read the side of a cereal box. Her presence was so powerful and momentous."[1]

Having been silent for so many years may have contributed to Angelou's belief in the power of words. While entertaining or hosting a gathering in her home, if she hears a guest say something offensive or unwholesome, she will immediately gather that person's things and personally escort the offender out. She doesn't want corrupt, noxious language spoken in her presence and certainly not in her home. "It soaks into the upholstery," she says.[2]

It amazes me that a young girl who was silent during the years that most children are learning to communicate could grow to value language so and become such a master of it. Between the ages of seven and thirteen, we learn our foundation for communication. We learn correct pronunciation and inflection, how to build a sentence, read aloud, and memorize and recite Bible verses and poetry. Angelou endured these formative years in self-imposed silence. What is the mystery of her commanding ability with words?

She says, "For years I thought of my whole body as an ear."[3] All those years, she was *listening.*

Silence. Listening.

Maybe she was listening and studying the way others spoke

and evaluating what elements of each statement made it either powerful, mediocre, or meaningless. Perhaps she listened intently as some people used words to harm and others used words to inspire, all the while dissecting each remark. She may have listened to the tone of voice with which people spoke to one another and made note of how that could be respectful at one moment and condescending the next. Then I imagine her rehearsing in her mind how she would effectively use tone in her voice, if she chose to speak. She most likely heard other children or even adults make statements that were unwise or just plain ridiculous. She may have thought to herself, "It would have been wiser to say . . . ," or "How could I have said that to make the most impact?" or "How could that have been stated more succinctly?"

Silence. Listening. Wisdom.

Former French president Charles de Gaulle is noted for saying, "Silence is the ultimate weapon of power."[4] What is it about silence that would prompt a world leader to make such a statement? I believe the answer is, again, *listening.*

Silence. Listening. Wisdom. Power.

"Silence Is Weird," states a billboard for Cingular, the cellular telephone company. But God's Word says, "Even a fool is thought wise if he keeps silent, and discerning if he holds his tongue" (Proverbs 17:28).

A recent study shows that the average American household has a television turned on for seven hours each day and a radio that blares for four hours a day. We thrive on noise. I find myself with the TV turned on just for company, having no idea what is showing. I will not turn off the ringer on my telephone during my daily prayer time. I guess I think that someone may call with something more important than what God has to say to me. How crazy is that? As Job told his tormenting "counselors": "If only you would be altogether silent! For you, that would be wisdom" (Job 13:5).

If it is not the television, the phone, the radio, or the stereo, we fill in the dead air with chatter. Chatter, chatter, chatter. Yet

God's Word says, "When words are many, sin is not absent, but he who holds his tongue is wise" (Proverbs 10:19).

I wonder . . . even when God tells us over and over that silence is a sign of wisdom, why are we so afraid of it?

Scripture consistently equates silence with wisdom. The world consistently says silence is weird or uncomfortable. We must choose which one we will believe. While we are talking about opening our mouths in wisdom, we need to pay heed to *closing* our mouths in wisdom as well.

Silence enables us to hear—to hear what is going on around us, to hear what is going on inside us. Silence makes listening possible. For silence to produce wisdom, we must stop talking and start

- listening to others,
- listening to our own hearts and minds,
- and listening to the voice of God.

LISTENING TO OTHERS

Glenda moved into an apartment upstairs from me when she was a recent college graduate embarking on her first "real" job. She had landed a sales position with a leading pharmaceutical company, and one of the reasons she got this coveted job was her outgoing, bubbly personality. She could talk to anyone about anything at any time. In fact, she rarely stopped talking!

Glenda's company held an annual sales meeting at which she would get the opportunity to meet with the company's executives for the first time. What an honor. Right before she left to attend this meeting, her manager pulled her aside and advised her that she needed to not talk so much.

My precious friend came to me visibly upset, shaken, and worried. What did he mean—not talk so much? Did she really talk that much? She never thought her "gift for gab" would cause her to fear losing the job of her dreams. Knowing Glenda, I knew exactly what her manager was trying to tell her. I gave her a little card to keep with her on her trip. It said:

> *Even a fool is thought wise if he keeps silent,*
> *and discerning if he holds his tongue.*
>
> Proverbs 17:28

In the presence of such influential people as the CEO and the president of her company, it was wise for Glenda to listen more than she spoke. While she was usually engaging when she did speak, sometimes her words made her appear a bit ditzy. By knowing when to hold her tongue, Glenda would be considered wise.

The lesson here is: You may not be the sharpest tack in the box, but no one will know unless *you* tell them. Know when to hold your tongue and when to speak.

> Better to remain silent and be thought a fool than to open your mouth and remove all doubt.
>
> ANONYMOUS

An opposite example is Ben, a real mover and shaker. He was the CEO of a major construction firm until he took early retirement to pursue public service. He moved on to head government agencies and to be a governor's chief of staff before being appointed president of a major university. When an international manufacturing company's CEO stepped down, the board of directors called Ben. Now he is running another major corporation. I have studied Ben, trying to figure out his secret to success. One thing I have noticed is that he doesn't talk much, but he listens very intently. In fact, he often makes me very self-conscious even when he is across the room and presumably engaged in another conversation altogether. I know he is listening.

When I was working in sales, I went through countless hours of training. In one such course, we were challenged to identify the "fox" in each presented sales scenario. The "fox" was the customer who was the ultimate decision maker. That person held the power to determine my fate as a vendor for that company. The primary defining characteristic of the "fox" was his or her silence. Often it was the person who slipped into the meeting at the last minute, sat in the back of the room, and just listened.

Silence. Listening. Wisdom. Power. Get the connection?

In August 2000, a college freshman named Brett Banfe vowed to not speak for an entire year. His idea to keep silent came about when he and a friend were debating about how long they could go without talking. Banfe's friend told him there was no way he could go a whole year without talking. Yet he did it. After 371 days of silence, Banfe told reporters that before this experience, "I'm embarrassed to say, almost, that I wouldn't listen to people if they talked. I'd wait for them to stop talking, then I'd start talking. Because . . . my opinion was the right one anyway. . . . So I think the one area I'll transform is how I listen to people."[5]

Listening.

I am telling you, ladies, this is a life-changing truth. Remember the safety rule we were taught in grammar school? *Stop, Look, and Listen.* Stop talking, look others in the eye, and really listen to what they have to say. If you will apply this principle in your interaction with other people, it will revolutionize your relationships.

LISTENING TO YOUR OWN HEART AND MIND

Pinocchio had Jiminy Cricket. He was tangible, spoke audibly, and would jump in Pinoc's face if he was acting crazy. Still, Pinocchio was too busy to hear him when it really mattered. Look where it got him! It is unfortunate, but in the real world the Blue Fairy doesn't dress up a wandering cricket to play conscience for each of us. We have to listen to our own hearts and minds.

Some might call listening to yourself "meditating." That is probably a really good term, although meditation has been given a bad rap in this day of New Age philosophy. For Christians, meditation is not "emptying your head." It is actually the reverse. It is really *thinking*. I am not talking about a spiritual urging or the Holy Spirit speaking to you. We will cover that shortly. Right now I am talking about using your head. God gave you a brain and a heart. You need to stop talking for a minute and use those precious gifts.

At Marquette University High School in Milwaukee, each day during the season of Lent the whole school pauses for three minutes of silent reflection. Just before sixth period, a faculty member announces over the intercom the theme for the day, like "think of something for which you are grateful." Then for three minutes there is no talking, no giggling, no phones ringing, nothing.[6]

This exercise is based on the teaching of St. Ignatius, founder of the Jesuit order of priests. The idea is to silence yourself, take inventory of how your day is going, and plan what is left of it in a thoughtful way.

The average American woman of the twenty-first century seems to be running around like a chicken with its head cut off. How often do we say, "I can't even hear myself think"? Do we ever just stop for a moment and thoughtfully plan our days? Do we ever pause to think of how we can best use our time to glorify God? Very rarely, I believe.

I guarantee that the abundant life Jesus came to provide for us does not mean a life filled with as many activities as possible. That is not the kind of abundance Christ intended. He purposed for us to have a life that was rich and full of meaning. To achieve that level of significance, we have got to stop talking, stop running, and start thoughtfully considering how we steward our time, our days, our lives.

One vital discipline that can be classified as listening to our own hearts and minds is my friend Julie's "fast-forward thinking" philosophy. This is the practice of considering the consequences of a particular action before we proceed with it. It might mean thinking, "If I say _____, how am I going to feel afterward? Will I wish I hadn't said it?" It may mean thinking, "If I follow the crowd and jump off this cliff, what will be the consequences? I will be crushed on the rocks below. Oh, maybe that is not such a good idea after all." Or, "If I don't calm down before I talk to my child, what will happen? I will be screaming like a maniac, and 'man's anger does not bring about the righteous life that God desires,' and then I will regret talking in anger. So maybe I better cool off first." Whatever it is, fast-forward thinking cannot happen unless we take the time to be silent and listen.

Another advantage of being silent is to be able to think of just the right thing to say. If we can just slow down and allow a moment of silence, we can think of what we want to say and the best way to say it. This makes for wise speech.

LISTENING TO THE VOICE OF GOD

In the silence of the early morning, I see the mist rising in the woods outside the window of my special room. This is my time to commune with God. Many times in those quiet moments I read my Bible. Other times I pray. Usually when I pray, I write my prayers in a journal. When the Holy Spirit gives rise to important thoughts, I write them down as well.

God speaks to us in the silence:

> "Pay attention, Job, and listen to me;
> be silent, and I will speak. . . .
> be silent, and I will teach you wisdom."
> Job 33:31, 33

He waits until we are listening. King David was a pretty busy guy. Yet he waited in silence to hear from God:

My soul waits in silence for God only;
From Him is my salvation.
Psalm 62:1 (NASB)

To know God, we must listen to Him. We must be willing to wait in silence for Him. He holds all the answers.

A defining moment in my life came during the summer before I started the fifth grade. I spent a week at a missions camp in southern Oklahoma. One evening during the worship service, as I stood in silence praying, God spoke to me. He told me He had a plan for my life and that plan included ministry. That moment stayed in the back of my mind for years. I have often wondered why, as an eleven-year-old girl, I would think God had spoken to me. And then why would I still be reliving and rethinking the experience decades later?

Then came another defining moment. More than twenty years had passed. I was pregnant with my son. I realized that, like it or not, this child would have a major impact on my career, which had been the primary focus of my life until this point. I cried, "What in the world am I going to do, God? Why have you brought me to this place?" There, alone in the silence of our tiny bedroom, on my knees, I heard God's voice again: "Rhonda, you know I have a plan for you. I want you to minister to others. I am in charge. Don't worry." If not for that silent moment, I might not be writing this sentence at this moment.

Ladies, just be quiet. Rest in the Lord. Listen to Him. He will speak to you.

"Be still, and know that I am God."
Psalm 46:10

SUMMARY

Silence is a virtue. It is powerful. It is a manifestation of wisdom, of prudence. Yet, having said all that, I must add that sometimes silence is absolutely unacceptable. Silence is inappropriate when a child needs to hear, "Good job" or "I am proud of you"; when another needs to hear, "You are precious to me"; or when your husband needs to hear, "I love you" or "I appreciate you."

To be like the wise, worthy woman of Proverbs 31, to be a woman who glorifies the Father, we must discern when silence is appropriate and even required, but also when it is unacceptable. Listen to those around you. Listen to your heart. Listen to the voice of God.

> *There is a time for everything,*
> *and a season for every activity under heaven: . . .*
> *a time to be silent and a time to speak.*
>
> Ecclesiastes 3:1, 7

⚜ 7 ⚜
I've Told You Time and Time Again
Stop Complaining, Start Trusting

· · · · · · · · · · · · · ·

Do everything without complaining or arguing.

PHILIPPIANS 2:14

O ur first home was a darling old brick, fairy-tale cottage with green shutters; a beautiful, manicured lawn brimming with glorious lavender and scarlet blossoms; and what else but a picket fence. It was meticulously decorated and so cozy for a newly married couple. It was perfect . . . except for a leaky roof over a small, snug den, which was added by the previous owner. Whenever it rained, our breakfast area and den were an obstacle course of pots and pans, towels and buckets. The constant dripping was so incredibly annoying that it was almost impossible to exist in that part of the house. The incessant drip-drip-drip, plip-plop-plip-plop ceaselessly echoed in our ears. Nothing could control it, short of replacing the entire roof. We were constantly hoisting heavy, sopping wet towels, replacing them with dry ones, only to have to replace them yet again in what seemed like seconds. Wringing towels, emptying buckets, stalking each new leak, plip-plop-plip-plop . . . stop the madness!

> *A constant dripping on a day of steady rain*
> *And a contentious woman are alike.*
> Proverbs 27:15 (NASB)

Is this what your family thinks it is like to live with you? "But I am not contentious," you may protest. Are you sure?

WHAT IS A CONTENTIOUS WOMAN?

Are you critical of others? Are you a complainer? Are you a nag? Are you a whiner? If you answered no to all of those questions, ask your kids, your husband, your parents, or your roommate. If they answer no, read this chapter anyway. (They may just be afraid of you!)

With his deluxe assortment of wives, Solomon must have known this kind of woman firsthand:

> *It is better to dwell in a corner of the house top, than with a brawling woman in a wide house.*
> Proverbs 21:9 (KJV)

He wrote that one twice (see 25:24). Solomon must have spent some nights on the roof! From the roof, he seems to have fled to the desert:

> *Better to live in a desert*
> *than with a quarrelsome and ill-tempered wife.*
> Proverbs 21:19

The words *quarrelsome* and *brawling* used in these verses are the Hebrew words *madon* and *kaas,* which mean to judge, contend, or plead; to cause or stir up grief; to provoke to anger.[1] Simply put, Solomon is describing a woman who is critical, complaining, and a nag!

A Contentious Woman Is Critical

Once upon a time in a faraway land lived a beautiful princess named Michal. She was in love with a peasant boy named David, who, although poor, was brave and strong. Michal's father, King Saul, promised David he could marry her if he would bring back the foreskins of a hundred of their archenemies. David so loved Michal that he returned with two hundred! (He really, really, really wanted her!)

The two were married, but they did not live happily ever after. The king became jealous of David's popularity and decided to have him killed. Michal helped him escape, but she would not leave the comfort of the palace to be with him.

Years later, after Saul died, David returned to become king. Michal became queen. She had grown bitter and hard and was more in love with her status as queen and her luxurious surroundings than with the man who once was her hero.

David's country's most cherished treasure had been stolen, and when he retrieved it, there was great celebration. David danced in the streets with his people as the queen looked on from her window. When David went home to celebrate with his beloved, there was no hero's welcome. Instead, Michal criticized David. "Have you no sense of decorum? You looked like a fool dancing half-naked in the streets with those commoners! You are the king! You have a certain image to uphold. Are you just trying to embarrass me?"

On David's most victorious day, Michal was critical of him. For that she paid dearly. Her marriage was never the same after that, and she never bore an heir to the throne.[2]

Do you seem to find fault in everyone around you? Is everything that goes wrong in your life someone else's fault? Is your pastor not preaching just right? Is the worship service too contemporary? Is Tom a horrible Bible study leader? Is Rebecca a bad driver? Does your son always need a haircut? Is your daughter's house not quite clean enough? Surely you taught her better than that!

If you recognize yourself in any of these criticisms, take to heart Jesus' counsel:

> *"Do not judge, or you too will be judged. For in the same way you judge others, you will be judged, and with the measure you use, it will be measured to you.*
>
> *"Why do you look at the speck of sawdust in your brother's eye and pay no attention to the plank in your own eye? How can you say to your brother, 'Let me take the speck out of your eye,' when all the time there is a plank in your own eye? You hypocrite, first take the plank out of your own eye, and then you will see clearly to remove the speck from your brother's eye."*
>
> Matthew 7:1–5

This is a major life lesson. We have absolutely no authority to criticize or condemn one another. We are accountable to God for those planks in our own eyes. Dealing with them is a full-time job. So we really don't have time to worry about the sins of others.

If Michal had spent her efforts dissecting and disposing of her own sin, splinter by splinter, rather than trying to find fault with her husband, her life would have had a completely different outcome. She would have been remembered as a godly woman instead of a bitter woman. She could have given birth to the future king of Israel, a forefather of the Messiah. In light of this, can we afford the consequences of not dealing with our own sin?

Jesus said, "If any one of you is without sin, let him be the first to throw a stone at her" (John 8:7). When, or *if*, you ever become without sin yourself, then you can judge or criticize another. Until then, clean your own house.

A Contentious Woman Is a Complainer

The first time my friend Val went snow skiing, it was not a pleasant experience for her. She was cold and wet, and skiing was rather frightening. We gave her a T-shirt on that trip which said "Cry Baby" on it. It listed all the complaints that you could possibly hear from a new skier on the mountain. Val is not a complainer under normal circumstances, but in this extreme situation, she was not a happy camper!

Are you a crybaby? "It's too hot." "It's too cold." "I have a headache." "I don't like spaghetti." "I wish I had a nicer house." "I need a new car." "I'm hungry." "I'm thirsty." "I want a swimming pool." "My foot hurts." "The living room needs painting." "This bed is lumpy."

The children of Israel complained about everything. All through Exodus and Numbers you can read about their perpetual whining. God delivered them out of slavery in Egypt, yet they complained that they were better off being slaves than being in the desert and hungry. God provided food for them every day in the wilderness, yet they complained that they were bored with the taste.

How could these people, who had witnessed God parting the Red Sea, who had been led by a pillar of fire at night and shaded by a cloud in the day, who had awakened every morning to find just the right amount of food for that day, still doubt God and complain? It's unfathomable. What does it take, folks?

But aren't we just like them? Like the children of Israel, when we complain, we doubt God's sovereignty. We question His authority over our lives, over this earth. We are apparently skeptical of His love for us. If we trusted Him, we would not have to complain. We could pray about our needs instead and have confidence that God will take care of us.

A Contentious Woman Is a Nag

A nag gripes about the same thing over and over and over. Wives are notorious for nagging their husbands, but we can also nag our children, our parents, and our friends.

If your loved ones were to give you a T-shirt, what would be written on it? Would it say "Take Out the Trash" in big block letters? If it did, would that save you the energy of saying it yet again?

First Corinthians 13:5 says, "Love does not demand its own way" (TLB). If you are habitually harping around your house, you are demanding your own way. You are a nag.

If you must ask your husband to do something for you, just ask once. Ask nicely. If he doesn't take care of that particular need, so be it. You do the right thing by obeying God and not complaining. Then trust God to handle the rest. God may choose to convict your husband that he is not doing what he should. Or God may choose to convict you that you never should have asked him to do it in the first place. Either way, trust God to handle it. Nagging is the same as not trusting God.

I have struggled with nagging in my marriage too. Between our kitchen and our den we have a breakfast bar. Because of its central location, my husband's things seem to accumulate there. Tonight the bar is littered with an old newspaper, a printed e-mail message, miscellaneous opened mail, a tape recorder, a video camera, a number of Post-it notes with various reminders, an old name tag (not his—who is Judy?), a stack of charts and files, an empty plastic toolbox, a cell phone, and a pager.

Having to look at this clutter all day long every day would drive many women nuts! It drove me nuts for years. I complained about it continually. Worse than that, I would sometimes try to clean it up for him.

Then, one day, I figured out that this is just the way Jimmy works. He cleans it up whenever we are expecting guests, and if guests arrive unexpectedly, then so what—they can see the mess. His happiness is much more valuable to me than seeing my bar clean. Asking him over and over to clean it up will only make him unhappy and cause friction in our home.

The same applies to any person and any situation. Are you always ragging on your kids about cleaning their rooms or combing their hair? How about your roommate, if you have one? Are you continually after her about running the vacuum? Does she ever say, "Hey, get off my back"? That would be a good sign that you are nagging.

My husband likes me to keep a to-do list for him. He welcomes the reminder on paper. By making him a list and leaving it in the appointed place, I avoid nagging.

Make your need or request known only once. Then trust God to take care of the rest. If your need or desire is not fulfilled, either God knows that you do not really need it or that you can handle it yourself. Whatever the case, it may not be for you to know or understand. Still, God promises that He will take care of you. Trust Him!

THE ROOT OF ALL CONTENTION

At the root of all whining, complaining, nagging, and criticism is one basic error: We are seeking our fulfillment and contentment from something or someone besides God.

If we count on our children to fulfill us, we will never be satisfied with their performance. It will never be enough. They will never love us enough. They will never adequately appreciate the nine long months we carried them in our womb. They will never value enough those endless hours of labor we endured to bring them into the world.

If we depend on our husband to make us happy and contented, we will never be happy with him either. He will always forget a birthday or anniversary. He will always be late for dinner. He will never appreciate our slaving over a hot stove to provide him with a delicious dinner. We will nag, berate, and criticize him until he is filled with resentment. We might even drive him away.

If you think this will never happen to you, think again. In a previous chapter, I told you about my friend Jean who complained and nagged her way directly to divorce court. Her husband just couldn't take any more. Jean was depending on her husband to make her feel secure, valuable, beautiful, and special.

He could never do quite enough to make her happy. Jean then ran to her parents for support. But she soon realized that not even they could provide the amount of love and nurturing she needed to make her feel fulfilled.

I have seen this happen in marriages all around me. I started to wonder, "What is it about my marriage that makes me so much happier?" I realized that it was not my marriage exactly, but the fact that I do not depend on my husband as the sole provider of my happiness. The answer is that I am actively seeking God. I know He is in control of my life. I know He is sovereign. I know He is the source of my strength and happiness. I know He values me so much that He sent His Son to die for me. That makes me pretty special.

Besides making me terribly content in my circumstances, my faith in God is also a huge relief to my husband. It allows him to spend his efforts wisely and seek the Lord as well, instead of spinning his wheels trying to make me happy.

Seeking the Lord is the only way to truly live, as the prophet Amos proclaimed:

> *This is what the LORD says to the house of Israel:*
> *"Seek me and live;*
> *do not seek Bethel,*
> *do not go to Gilgal,*
> *do not journey to Beersheba.*
> *For Gilgal will surely go into exile,*
> *and Bethel will be reduced to nothing."*
> *Seek the LORD and live,*
> *or he will sweep through the house of Joseph like a fire;*
> *it will devour,*
> *and Bethel will have no one to quench it.*
> Amos 5:4–6

"Seek the Lord and live." That suggests to me that if you are not seeking God, you are not really living. If you want to live—

to really live—if you want to love life and be truly content, seek God. Find your fulfillment in Him first and foremost.

THE FIX FOR ALL COMPLAINTS

If you can't trust God to take care of you, you will never stop complaining, arguing, griping, and whining about everything. Seek God and trust His provision:

"So do not worry, saying, 'What shall we eat?' or 'What shall we drink?' or 'What shall we wear?' For the pagans run after all these things, and your heavenly Father knows that you need them. But seek first his kingdom and his righteousness, and all these things will be given to you as well."

Matthew 6:31–33

I recently received an e-mail with the following message:

Rules to live by:

Live simply.

Give more.

Expect less.

When I read that I thought, if we lived by those rules, we would certainly not complain as much as we do. I was inspired to develop my own set of rules especially for potentially contentious women. I realize that sometimes a genuine need must be communicated to another person. If I need my husband to change a light bulb in a fixture that I cannot reach, it would be foolish to expect him to read my mind. It would also be foolish for me to pray that the Holy Spirit would inspire him to change the light bulb without my asking. In cases like these, I refer to the following set of guidelines to assure I don't reach contentiousness.

Rhonda's Rules for
Potentially Contentious Women

1. Take your case to God.
2. State your case only to the individual responsible for the issue.
3. State your case only if you are willing to help resolve the issue.
4. State your case gently and humbly.
5. State your case only once.
6. Trust God.

Let's look at each of these in some detail.

1. Take Your Case to God

How often do we say as a last resort, "I guess all there is left to do is pray about it"? We should always go to the Lord first.

Another reason that we should pray about our needs is that, if it is not a need we can talk to God about, it is probably not something we really need. For example: If I am asking Jimmy to change a light bulb that is well within my reach, but I just don't want to change it, do you think I would feel justified asking God about it? Of course not! I would be embarrassed to take this to God, because I am just being lazy.

If we can take our need to the Father in prayer, He will validate it. He will say, "This is a real need. You should ask Jimmy to help you with it." God might also say, "Rhonda, you can easily take care of this yourself. Stop being so lazy."

Before you even think about complaining to another human being, pray. If God validates your need, then you can proceed to the next step.

2. State Your Case Only to the Individual Responsible for the Issue

If I need a light bulb changed in my house, what good will

it do to complain to all my friends about it? "Jimmy hasn't changed the light bulb in the den. It has been out for weeks now."

The way to get it resolved is to appeal directly to my husband. He is the only one who is truly responsible for fixing the light bulb problem. If I complain to everyone else but never talk to him about it, I am only going to make him angry (and I may never get the light bulb changed!).

The children of Israel were guilty of this. In Numbers 11, they grumbled to each other about the food situation. What did that accomplish? Moses took his complaint directly to the One responsible for taking care of this need: God. God honored Moses' request but was angry with the people.

3. State Your Case Only If You Are Willing to Help Resolve the Issue

If I ask Jimmy to change the light bulb and he tries to but no bulbs are in the cupboard, then I should be willing to purchase light bulbs the next time I go to the store. What if I just said, "You're on your own, buddy"? Am I ever going to get that bulb replaced? No. Am I stirring up strife in my home? Yes. I would be a contentious woman.

4. State Your Case Gently and Humbly

What if I went to Jimmy and growled, "You lazy bum. That light bulb has been out for weeks. You are the light bulb replacer in this house. What is your problem?" What kind of woman would speak to her husband like that? I will give you a hint. It starts with a *C.*

What if I asked him instead, "Honey, when you get a chance, could you replace that bulb? I put a new bulb on your desk so you don't have to search for it. I would really appreciate it." By treating him with respect and being pleasant about my request, I would have a very good chance of finally getting this bulb replaced. The book of Proverbs encourages us to take this approach:

Through patience a ruler can be persuaded,
and a gentle tongue can break a bone.
Proverbs 25:15

The wise in heart are called discerning,
and pleasant words promote instruction.
Proverbs 16:21

A gentle answer turns away wrath,
but a harsh word stirs up anger.
Proverbs 15:1

Your words will be more persuasive if they are gentle and pleasant.

5. State Your Case Only Once

We have already explained nagging. If I perpetually remind Jimmy every day that the light bulb is out and he needs to replace it, he is going to wish he lived on the corner of the roof instead of staying warm and dry inside with me.

But if I ask him only once and put it on his list of to-dos, I have done my part. He will get to it when he can. I can trust God to convict him, or we can just live with a dark den. Honestly, my husband's happiness and the health of my marriage are much more important to me than the amount of light in my den.

Bottom line: When you nag, you are telling the recipient that your happiness is more important than his happiness. When you badger your husband, you are telling him that your need or want is more important than his happiness or the health of your marriage.

6. Trust God

It all comes down to trusting God. If it is truly my husband's responsibility to change the light bulb, then he is ultimately accountable to God to change it. I can rest in knowing that God knows just the amount of light we need in our den and also just the right time for my husband to fit the job into his schedule. I have no need to worry about it. Trust God.

Let's try these rules out in another example, with which I bet you can identify. Let's say that you feel your church's worship service is just too contemporary. What do you do? Do you go to all of your friends and say, "The worship service was too loud and contemporary Sunday, didn't you think?"

A wise woman would:

1. Take it to the Lord. Pray about it.

2. If God leads you to take your concerns further, you should not talk to your friends about it. You should take your comments to your church's pastor in charge of music. He is the one who is responsible for it.

3. Are you willing to help resolve the issue? Are you willing to join the worship service planning committee? Are you willing to join the choir or worship team? Are you willing to pray with the worship leader regarding this matter?

4. Talk to your music pastor gently and humbly. God has placed him in a position of authority in your church. No matter how distraught you are regarding the level of noise you endured Sunday morning, you are to address him with respect. Also, your words will be more persuasive if they are gentle.

5. I guarantee you that if you tell your church's worship leader once that the song selection needs to include some old hymns, that will be enough. He will either make the change, or he won't. There is no need to belabor the point.

6. Trust God that He is ultimately in control of your church's worship services. He is, you know.

OUR ULTIMATE EXAMPLE

If we aren't ready to stop criticizing, whining, and complaining yet, then this is the clincher!

Let us fix our eyes on Jesus, the author and perfecter of our faith, who for the joy set before him endured the cross, scorning its shame, and sat down at the right hand of the throne of God.

Hebrews 12:2

To this you were called, because Christ suffered for you, leaving you an example, that you should follow in his steps.
  "He committed no sin,
    and no deceit was found in his mouth."
When they hurled their insults at him, he did not retaliate; when he suffered, he made no threats. Instead, he entrusted himself to him who judges justly.

1 Peter 2:21–23

Jesus Christ is our ultimate example. He endured the shame and the pain of death on a cross. He endured insults, but He didn't repay in kind. He suffered, yet He did not criticize or complain. He did not lash out at His offenders or cry out for mercy. Not once. Instead, He quietly trusted the Father's plan, knowing the ultimate result would secure our redemption.

He did it for you.

I believe that Jesus takes our complaining very personally. He must think, "How petty of her. How ungrateful she is. How can she complain about such meaningless little things when I died for her without a word?"

Think about it.

Are you a contentious woman? Are you critical, complaining, or a nag?

> *A constant dripping on a day of steady rain*
> *And a contentious woman are alike.*
> Proverbs 27:15 (NASB)

Be grateful to the Lord. Trust the Father, or be like constant dripping! Come on, don't be a drip!

8

God Bless You
Speaking a Blessing to Others

. . . .

Therefore encourage one another
and build each other up,
just as in fact you are doing.

1 THESSALONIANS 5:11

Whenever someone sneezes, we always say, "Bless you" or "God bless you." When my infant daughter, Scout, sneezes, she sneezes three times consecutively, without fail. Dainty, diminutive, "Achoo, achoo, achoo." Everyone within earshot unconsciously repeats, "Bless you. Bless you. Bless you."

I believe Christians are commanded to bless one another at all times—not just when someone sneezes! How do we bless others? Through encouraging and uplifting them, as Paul says:

> *Therefore encourage one another and build each other up,*
> *just as in fact you are doing.*
>   1 Thessalonians 5:11

Who is included in "one another"? Our husbands, children, fellow believers, parents, and even our adversaries.

BLESSING YOUR HUSBAND

Gary Chapman is a noted marriage counselor who discovered that people give and receive love in five basic ways. Chapman calls these the "Five Love Languages." The first love language is "Words of Affirmation," which would be encouraging words, kind words, and humble words.[1]

Encouraging Words

The word *encourage* means "to inspire courage."[2] How can we inspire courage in our husbands? We can visualize them tired and dragging after a hard day's work. Then picture them standing tall and proud, smiling, chin held high, and chest puffing out. Next, ask yourself, "What can I say to him that will effect this energized transition?"

You can tell him how fully you appreciate him, his generosity, his hospitality, his helpfulness, his faithfulness, and his leadership. If you find yourself hard-pressed to produce words of inspiration out of the blue, make a list of what you appreciate about him. This will facilitate your blessing him. For example, list the valuable jobs he does around the house. List the ways he shows kindness to others. List his attractive physical characteristics. You could even sneak a peek at your list as your husband pulls into the driveway in the evening and surprise him with encouragement:

- "Thank you for taking the kids to school today."
- "Thank you for putting gas in the car."
- "I appreciate how you helped Mrs. Jones next door with her lawn."
- "You have the most beautiful eyes."
- "You are so handsome."
- "I love your haircut."
- "I am proud to be your wife."
- "I am glad we are married."

These words voiced with sincerity will invigorate your husband. Another way of blessing him is supporting and cheering him on in achieving a particular goal or pursuing a favorite hobby. If he really loves to build things, encourage him in doing that. "Honey, you are so good at building things!" "That shelf you made in the garage looks great!" If he basks in the sportsman's world of camouflage gear and tree stands, assure him of your approval. Praise his skill as a marksman and hunter. Marvel at the beauty of the pheasant or the enormity of the deer's antlers. Thank him for putting meat on the table. (He will love that!) If he dreams of writing, tell him he should pursue that dream: "I know you can do it."

Kind Words

Speaking kind words has a lot to do with our tone of voice and inflection. The same request can be imparted either graciously or ruthlessly. Graciously: "Dear, could you please take out the garbage this evening?" Ruthlessly: "Do you think you could take out the garbage *this* evening?"

Speaking kindly, charitably, and affirmingly to our husbands requires empathy. Ask yourself, "How is he feeling right now?" "What does he need from me?" "If I were in his shoes, what would I need to hear right now?"

It is crucial that we speak kind words to our husbands. Our understanding and compassion are like a warm hearth glowing on an endless winter day. In other words, they will make him want to come home.

Humble Words

Humble words build up others instead of tearing them down. If we say, "Thank you so much for taking the garbage out tonight," but then add, "It's about time"—we might as well hit him over the head with an iron skillet.

Encourage your husband. Speak a blessing to him. Declare your gratitude and praise. Proclaim his winsomeness, his machismo, his fortitude. Profess your devotion to him, your passion for him, and your unceasing love. Don't be concerned with overindulging him! Your home will be more peaceful; your marriage, more joyful; and your husband, euphoric.

As his "suitable helper," your words of encouragement and affirmation are markedly more powerful and influential than those of anyone else. He needs to hear *your* admiration, *your* praise, and *your* undying support of him.

BLESSING YOUR CHILDREN

Blessing your children with your words is crucial as well, especially if their primary love language is "words of affirmation." Even if you do not have children of your own, you may have nieces, nephews, or younger siblings that need a blessing from you. The fundamental words each child needs to hear are "I love you." However, you must speak your love in other words as well.

As Solomon reveals, "The tongue has the power of life and death" (Proverbs 18:21). Our words can speak life to a child, or they can speak death. Words that speak life are words of affection, praise, encouragement, and guidance.

Involving Dad

One crucial and often forgotten means of blessing your children is to love your husband and exhort him in his relationship with them. A study by sociologist Kathleen Harris found that the more time children spent with their fathers, the more education the children completed. Also, the stronger the emotional bond between children and their fathers, the less likely the children were to engage in delinquent behavior.[3]

Don't carp on him about spending time with the kids: "You never take the kids anywhere," or "You never spend any time with the kids." Instead, reassure him by pointing out his successes. "Sarah loved your 'date night' last weekend. You should do it more often." "Billy told me he had so much fun playing tennis with you the other night. Spending time with you is really special to him."

Words of Affection

Affectionate words show appreciation for who your child is and are not associated with performance. Several months ago, I started a ritual with my son when I put him to bed at night. When I tuck him in, I ask him, "How do you suppose that out of all the boys in all the world, God gave me the most precious one of all?" Frequently he rolls his eyes and says with a bashful grin, "Mom, you ask me that every night." Yet, I know that at least one time each day, I let him know that I treasure him.

Another way to express value and affection to your children is to read books with them that help you express your feelings. Max Lucado has written a series of children's books that help children understand their value to God and to their parents. In *Just In Case You Ever Wonder,* Lucado writes, "As you grow and change, some things will stay the same. I'll always love you. I'll always hug you. I'll always be on your side. And I want you to know that . . . just in case you ever wonder."

Reading these words to children, then saying, "I feel that way about you. Did you know that?" is a great way to convey that you treasure them, that you will always love them, that you will always be on their side.

One night when I was giving little Jimmy a bath, we were talking about how he had spoken disrespectfully to his daddy that day. His response to this discussion was, "I don't think I am the right boy for you." Oh, how my heart ached. I said, "You *are* the right boy for us. Daddy and I love you so much. God made you to be my boy. He gave you to us, and I thank him every day. But God also gave me the job of teaching you to speak respectfully. All boys have to learn to speak respectfully. You *are* the right boy, the most precious boy in the world." He needs to know, without a doubt, that he is the right boy for us. Expressing words of affection is one great way to remind him.

Words of Praise

Words of praise are different from words of affection in that they are praise for what a child does. This could be appreciation for clearing the table after dinner. Or saying, "Good job," for hitting the ball in a game, or roaring an unrestrained "Woo-hoo!" It could be telling your child that you see how hard he or she is working to excel in a particular subject at school. When children do something well, they need to hear from you that you noticed. They need to *hear* that you are proud of them.

A close friend in high school seemed to be the most confident, self-assured guy in the western hemisphere. His parents attended every ball game, every extracurricular activity. Every time he sang, played, or did anything, they were present. However, they did not believe in applauding him with words of praise. Doing so might make him arrogant, they thought.

When this young man became an adult, he was incredibly insecure. He pursued any kind of occupation that would put him on stage or in the limelight so his folks could come to watch him. This is the only way he ever got any approval from them. An audience was his drug of choice. Consequently, he never financially or emotionally provided for his own wife and children. Eventually, he lost them. He still appeared to be the most confident man around, but inside he was striving for some kind of praise, even though he would not admit to it until years later.

My parents always encouraged me to sing at church. They thought, and still believe, that I am the best singer in the world. They would tell me, "You should sing professionally!" I know that I am not the best singer in the world, nor do I have any secret, lofty musical ambitions. Still, knowing that my parents believed in my ability was and still is very important to me.

Lori was a stunningly beautiful young woman. Despite her striking appearance, she never believed that girl in the mirror was attractive at all. I remember visiting her grandmother one day and seeing Lori's photograph on the mantle. I said, "That is such a great picture." The grandmother said, "You know, Fern said the same thing just the other day. She went on and on about how pretty Lori is. I've never thought of her as being beautiful." I was amazed. No wonder my friend could never believe she was attractive.

Sincere words of praise, as opposed to empty flattery, are never wasted on children. Again, please don't concern yourself with overindulgence.

Words of Encouragement

As I was growing up, whenever I got into trouble or met with a challenge, my dad would say, "Rhonda Renee, you can do anything you set your mind to." As a kid, I guess I inadvertently absorbed his confidence, albeit reluctantly. I thought, "Yeah, yeah, yeah. All dads say that." "Sure, Daddy. Whatever."

However, one day when I was about twenty-six years old, it just sunk in. It occurred to me that I really could do anything I set my mind to do. To this day, honestly, I have no doubt that if I choose to succeed at something and am willing to work to accomplish it, I will succeed. I am certain that this attitude is 100 percent attributable to my dad's words of encouragement echoed over and over and over and over.

So encourage your children in their endeavors. Praise their accomplishments. Believe in them. Speak your confidence in them. Speak life.

Words of Guidance

As a parent, you are required to "train a child in the way he should go, and when he is old he will not turn from it" (Proverbs 22:6). Training includes words of guidance. These are not necessarily "don'ts"—"Don't do this. Don't do that." They may be conversations about values, about making right decisions. Several advertisements on television encourage parents to talk to their kids about drugs and smoking. Those conversations are crucial and build up your children. Engaging children in dialogue about sex and purity is especially important these days. (Talk about the power of life or death!)

Reading aloud books that express words of guidance provides an incredible opportunity for discussion. A particularly appropriate book for parents of preschool and early grade school children is Jennie Bishop's *The Princess and the Kiss*. It is the story of a princess who is given the most valuable gift at birth by God—her first kiss. Her parents keep the priceless kiss safe for her until she is old enough to appreciate its value. Then, as suitors come to court her, she considers if each one is worthy of such a precious gift as her kiss. This book is a great way to speak words of guidance and open paths of communication with children about the preciousness of purity.

As you go through each day, consider how you can communicate a blessing to your children. Ask yourself, "How can I use words of affection? How can I use words of praise? How can I use words of encouragement? How can I use words of guidance to inspire courage, to bless them?"

> *Behold, children are a gift of the Lord,*
> *The fruit of the womb is a reward.*
>
> Psalm 127:3 (NASB)

Let them *hear* how dear, how priceless, how treasured they truly are.

BLESSING YOUR PARENTS

Have you ever thought about blessing your parents? Our heavenly Father expects us to honor our earthly parents:

> *"Honor your father and mother"—which is the first commandment with a promise—"that it may go well with you and that you may enjoy long life on the earth."*
>
> Ephesians 6:2–3

Let me point out a few things that verse does not say. It does not say, "Honor your father and mother *only when you are a child.*" It does not say, "Honor your father and mother *if they let you do whatever you want.*" It does not say, "Honor your father and mother *if they deserve it*"!

It *does* say, "Honor your father and mother," period. Then there is a promise: "that it may go well with you and that you may enjoy long life on the earth." I believe that living the abundant life here on earth is partially dependent on honoring our father and mother. Scripture promises that if we will just do that, things will go well for us, and we may *enjoy* a long life on the earth. This principle is so simple that many Christians overlook it.

So, practically, what does it mean to honor your father and mother with your words? I believe there are four ways of honoring our parents with our words—respectful words, words of appreciation, words of encouragement, and sharing memories.

Respectful Words

When we speak to our parents, our words and tone ought always to be respectful, regardless of our age. You may be thinking, "But my parents were cruel to me." "My parents abused me physically and/or emotionally." Even if they do not deserve your respect, it is your obligation as a Christian to honor them. You do not have to let them hurt you or your children. You do not even have to let them be a part of your life. You do, however, have to honor them.

Respectful words include basic etiquette—perhaps addressing them as "ma'am" or "sir" when answering questions. Always include "please" in a request.

Speaking respectfully also applies to speaking *about* your parents. As an eight-year-old girl, I spoke about my mother in a disrespectful manner. My friend Robyn called to invite me to the circus. My mom said I could not go. I told Robyn that my mom was "mean." What I did not know was my mother had picked up another extension to make a telephone call. She heard every word that I said. It really hurt her, and I remember the circumstances to this day.

As we grow older and we learn that our parents are fallible, it is easier to speak of their failures or to call them old-fashioned or out of touch. Still, it is important that we remember to speak *of* our parents respectfully just as we speak *to* our parents respectfully.

Words of Appreciation

As a kid, did you tell your folks "thank you" for taking you to McDonalds or for driving you all over town to your various activities? Did you thank them for cooking meals and keeping a roof over your head? Did you thank them for working hard to provide an education for you? Did you thank them for taking you to church or for introducing you to the Lord?

Recently, I spoke to a group of mothers and daughters in Tulsa. I mentioned to the daughters that they could bless their mothers with their words simply by saying, "Thank you." I was amazed at the number of girls who told me they had really never considered thanking their mothers for all the things they do for them on a daily basis.

Even if you did not thank your parents as a kid, if they are still living, it is not too late. Seize the opportunity to thank them. "Thank you for taking me to church every Sunday." "Thank you for making sure I stayed in school." "Thank you for fixing pancakes all those Saturday mornings." There are very likely things about your childhood that you appreciate, that you took for granted as a kid, but now realize their significance. Thank your parents now. It will bless them.

Words of Encouragement

Saying, "I love you, Dad," or "I love you, Mom," becomes more and more important as your parents grow older. So many times I have heard of adult children who regret that they never told a parent how much they loved him or her before that parent died.

When my son tells me, "Mommy, you look really pretty," or "I sure do like you, Mommy," it truly warms my heart. How much greater will his words affect me when he is a thirty-year-old man?

Encouraging your parents is no different from encouraging your husband or children. Tell your mom how you admire the way she keeps her home so clean and comfortable. Tell your mom how you admire her knack for decorating. Tell your dad that you admire his ability to build things or that he is a great fisherman or golfer.

Sharing Memories

The most effective way to bless our parents verbally as we grow older is to share memories with them. "I was just remembering that crazy three-week vacation we took in the summer of '77! The air-conditioning went out with all four of us in the front seat of the pickup. And we had a great time anyway! Do you remember that song about Noah? I think we sang it in every state west of the Mississippi River!"

"Do you remember how we used to . . . " "It was so fun when you used to . . . when we were little." "When I was five, I thought you were the fastest and strongest dad in the whole world." "Do you remember shopping for that prom dress my senior year?"

Parents cherish remembering with you all the events that you experienced as a family. Share your favorite memories with them. It will truly be a blessing to them.

BLESSING OTHERS

Finally, all of you, live in harmony with one another; be sympathetic, love as brothers, be compassionate and humble. Do not repay evil with evil or insult with insult, but with blessing, **because to this you were called so that you may inherit a blessing.**

1 Peter 3:8–9 (emphasis added)

Godly men and women are commanded to encourage one another, to bless one another with their words. The primary way we can bless other Christians is by exhorting one another in our faith. Make a call or write a note to another believer. Tell her that you are praying for her. Tell her that you love her and that God loves her. Encourage her with Scripture. Encourage her to be the wife that God intends. Encourage her to be the mother that God intends. Encourage her to grow in the Lord.

Our words can speak life to all those around us.

BLESSING OUR ENEMIES

But I say unto you, Love your enemies, bless them that curse you, do good to them that hate you, and pray for them which despitefully use you, and persecute you.

Matthew 5:44 (KJV)

When someone hurts you intentionally, do not retaliate with rhetoric. Bless her instead. Compliment her dress. Commend her children. Ask who cuts her hair. You may have to stand there in silence for a moment while you conjure up a blessing for a particularly difficult individual. But do it. "Because to this you were called so that you may inherit a blessing."

SUMMARY

With your words, bless those around you—husband, children, parents, friends, acquaintances, strangers, and yes, even enemies. Wouldn't it be wonderful if others could say of you, "She always has something kind to say"? That you may inherit a blessing.

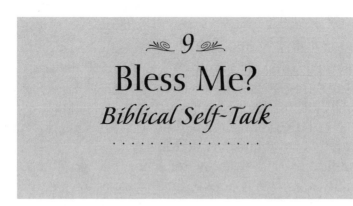

9

Bless Me?
Biblical Self-Talk

*I praise you because I am
fearfully and wonderfully made;
your works are wonderful,
I know that full well.*

PSALM 139:14

ach year in late summer my brother, Rob, would start "two-a-days" (high school football practices twice each day) and subsequently practice football late into the afternoon once school had begun in the fall. During my sixth- and seventh-grade years, I took over his paper route while he practiced ball. I rode the route on my purple, banana-seat bicycle with an enormous, ink-dirtied, canvas newspaper satchel strapped to my handlebars, tossing the day's news on neighbors' porches. My palms were jet-black and my face decorated with inky smudges.

One steaming August afternoon, the air felt like a damp dishrag on my skin, smothering any potential breath of fresh, cool oxygen. As I rounded the corner at the far end of Dana Drive, headed for a rare shred of shade to break the humidity's stranglehold if only for a moment, I realized I was talking out loud to myself. My first thought was, "Oh, my goodness! Did anyone see me talking to myself?" As I frantically searched my surroundings for potential spectators, I thought, "There you have it—the first sign you are going crazy is that you talk to yourself. I must be going crazy!" (I have no idea where I obtained this little tidbit of psychiatric wisdom.)

Thankfully, I have discovered since that we all talk to ourselves. Sometimes it is out loud, but most often silently.

THE POWER OF SELF-TALK

In an article for *Selfhelp Magazine* (online) in August 1998, Joe Kolezynski stated: "It has been established by psychologists and neuroscientists that every person in the world carries on an ongoing dialog, or self-talk, of between 150 to 300 words a minute. This works out to between 45,000 and 51,000 thoughts a day."[1]

While most of our self-talk is harmless, like, "I need to get milk at the grocery store," it can become fraught with danger when it takes on a negative slant.

> The ongoing negative reinforcement created by habitual negative self-talk results in the creation of a limiting belief(s) that goes on to become self-fulfilling prophecy.
> Beliefs—positive or negative—are literally etched into our brain in comfortable grooves or neural pathways. Incoming data from our senses travel on these neural pathways on the way to interpretation in the brain. Therefore, if you desire to change an unresourceful/limiting belief into an empowering belief, you must rewire the negative neural track created in the brain.[2]

This rewiring is accomplished with affirming self-talk. This concept of remapping our thinking is crucial in the training of world-class athletes. Sports psychologists train athletes to thwart negative beliefs by replacing them with thoughts that will lead to their desired outcome. Tiger Woods tells himself he is going to drive the golf ball 335 yards or that he is playing his best. An Olympic gymnast or figure skater tells herself she is at peak performance. She has prepared adequately for this event. She talks herself through her program as she has done hundreds of times before.

I use self-talk when I am skiing down a particularly challenging slope. As I stand at the summit, surveying the pitch of the powder before me and observing others crash and tumble their way down, I find myself thinking, "There is absolutely no way you are going to make it down this mountain alive." I have to stop myself and say, "Yes, I can do this. Tackle it one swoosh at a time." Then I start to the right, count to four and turn to the left, count to four and turn to the right, "two, three, four," repeating this process until I reach safety at the bottom.

SELF-TALK IN SCRIPTURE

You might be thinking, "So what does all this New Age psychobabble, mumbo jumbo have to do with me?" Well, it's not New Age, and it's not psychobabble. This same notion of rewiring neural pathways with affirming self-talk is spelled out in Scripture. It is an essential tool in every Christian's walk. Consider what Paul wrote to the Corinthian church:

We demolish arguments and every pretension that sets itself up against the knowledge of God, and **we take captive every thought to make it obedient to Christ.**

2 Corinthians 10:5 (emphasis added)

Capture your thoughts and test them to assure they are obedient to Christ. Then replace the rebel thoughts by renewing your mind with God's Word:

Do not conform any longer to the pattern of this world, but **be transformed by the renewing of your mind.** *Then you will be able to test and approve what God's will is—his good, pleasing and perfect will.*

Romans 12:2 (emphasis added)

Just as sports psychologists instruct athletes to stop destructive thoughts and supplant them with constructive convictions, so we Christians are to appraise every notion and renew our minds by bringing illegitimate thoughts under the authority of Scripture. God's Word gives a huge advantage to every believer. Instead of capturing the thought and rewiring it to achieve a result that we have imagined, we can replace our inaccurate thoughts with truth, God's Word, a firm foundation. His Word abundantly surpasses anything we could dream up (see Ephesians 3:20). When we believe something of ourselves that is not in line with Scripture, we can seize that thought, send it packing, and supersede it with truth.

Psychotherapists have been using this method for decades. In a certain form of therapy, with a psychologist's guidance an individual will actually carry on a conversation with his or her inner voice. The patient may even occupy one chair when asking questions and move to another chair to answer!

This is not hot-off-the-presses to Christian teaching. Kay Arthur utilizes this concept and calls it "letting your mind be renewed."[3] Beth Moore calls it "deprogramming and reprogramming," as well as "tearing down the lies" and "putting up the truth."[4] Martha Peace calls it the "put off/put on dynamic,"[5] putting off the wrong thought and putting on God's Word.

The basis for this teaching is that Christians of the twenty-first century (and every century before us) have been deceived by our world to believe things that are just not true of us. We are conditioned by worldly wisdom and even by the church to believe lies. Thus we live in bondage to those lies until we capture those controlling thoughts and replace them with God's Word.

Where do these erroneous beliefs come from? They come directly from the father of lies, Satan. If we have given our hearts to Christ, that means Satan has lost them. But he can still toy with our minds. Satan is prowling about looking for a weak, unaware moment to plant his deceit in our thoughts:

Be self-controlled and alert. Your enemy the devil prowls around like a roaring lion looking for someone to devour.

1 Peter 5:8

The International Standard Version says to stay "clear-minded and alert."

Submit yourselves, then, to God. Resist the devil, and he will flee from you. Come near to God and he will come near to you. Wash your hands, you sinners, and purify your hearts, you double-minded.

James 4:7–8

We absolutely must clear our minds of the junk that Satan plants in there. We must always be alert, never giving him an opening. The devil's strategy is to hold us in bondage to his fabrications and make us ineffective for building up God's kingdom. One of Satan's schemes is to distort the biblical balance of self-esteem, which is true humility. He will either cast doubt on the strength and righteousness we possess because of Christ, or he will trump up a sense of self-sufficiency—that we don't need God, that we are more important than others, that we deserve better or more than we have.

Paul warned the Christians in Rome about this:

For by the grace given me I say to every one of you: Do not think of yourself more highly than you ought, but rather think of yourself with sober judgment, in accordance with the measure of faith God has given you.

Romans 12:3

True humility "recognizes our strengths as well as our weaknesses and is not preoccupied with either."[6] People with a solid, biblical sense of self-esteem do not have to keep reminding others of their worth or their weaknesses and failures.

Stacy Colino, in an article titled "Six Ways To Boost Your Self-Confidence" in *Lifetime Online*, calls self-talk "brainwashing yourself."[7] I love this description. It makes me think, "Jesus does the stain-washing; I am responsible for the brain-washing." Through Christ's redemptive work on the cross, the stain of my sin is scrubbed clean. However, Satan can still attack my mind and tell me that I am worthless or keep me in bondage to his lies. I must renew my mind continually—brain-washing.

HOW TO WASH YOUR BRAIN

The process of brain-washing (renewing your mind) is a simple one:

1. Seize every thought.
2. Test each for authenticity to identify the lies that hold you in bondage.
3. Write out Scripture (on an index card) that represents God's truth opposing your specific stronghold. These will be the vehicles for creating those new neural pathways we talked about earlier.
4. Read your affirming Scripture (truth) aloud five to twenty times. (Continue doing this until you have succeeded in renewing your mind.)

Kolezynski suggests that you sit upright in a comfortable chair, relax, and speak your new resourceful thought aloud five to twenty times depending on your time constraints. He says, "By speaking your affirmation aloud you are down-stepping your thoughts to the brain's electrical network to speech, and you are involving more of your brain by including two more of your senses: auditory and kinesthetic."[8]

To help in this process, I've created the following chart that includes, in the first column, several common lies that Satan uses to render Christians unproductive. The second column lists Scriptures that spell out the truth. The third column provides remedy statements that incorporate the corrective truths of Scripture.

LIES WE BELIEVE	SCRIPTURE	THE TRUTH ABOUT ME
"I'm worthless."	"For you created my inmost being; you knit me together in my mother's womb. I praise you because I am fearfully and wonderfully made; your works are wonderful, I know that full well." (Psalm 139:13–14)	"I am an awesome work of God. God doesn't make worthless junk."
"My sin is too great. God cannot forgive me."	"If we confess our sins, he is faithful and just and will forgive us our sins and purify us from all unrighteousness." (1 John 1:9)	"If I confess my sin, He *will* forgive me."
"There is no reason for God to love me."	"For he chose us in him before the creation of the world to be holy and blameless in his sight. In love he predestined us to be adopted as his sons through Jesus Christ, in accordance with his pleasure and will." (Ephesians 1:4–5)	"The reason God loves me is because it makes Him happy. He loves me so much He adopted me. I am His child."

LIES WE BELIEVE	SCRIPTURE	THE TRUTH ABOUT ME
"God couldn't love me."	"For God so loved the world that he gave his one and only Son, that whoever believes in him shall not perish but have eternal life." (John 3:16)	"He loved me so much He sacrificed His only Son so I could live."
"I must disgust God."	"When I consider your heavens, the work of your fingers, the moon and the stars, which you have set in place, what is man that you are mindful of him, the son of man that you care for him? You made him a little lower than the heavenly beings and crowned him with glory and honor." (Psalm 8:3–5)	"I am precious to God."
"I don't have anything to offer."	"There are different kinds of gifts, but the same Spirit. There are different kinds of service, but the same Lord. There are different kinds of working, but the same God works all of them in all men. Now to each one the	"God has given me a gift through His Spirit to enable me to serve Him."

LIES WE BELIEVE	SCRIPTURE	THE TRUTH ABOUT ME
	manifestation of the Spirit is given for the common good." (1 Corinthians 12:4–7)	
"God has turned His back on me."	"Be strong and courageous. Do not be afraid or terrified because of them, for the LORD your God goes with you; he will never leave you nor forsake you." (Deuteronomy 31:6)	"God will never forsake me."
"I feel so alone."	"See that you do not look down on one of these little ones. For I tell you that their angels in heaven always see the face of my Father in heaven." (Matthew 18:10)	"Angels watch over me."
"God can never forgive my past."	"For I am convinced that neither death nor life, neither angels nor demons, neither the present nor the future, nor any powers, neither height nor depth, nor	"Nothing can separate me from God's love, not even my past!"

LIES WE BELIEVE	SCRIPTURE	THE TRUTH ABOUT ME
	anything else in all creation, will be able to separate us from the love of God that is in Christ Jesus our Lord." (Romans 8:38–39)	
"I will never be able to do enough to merit salvation."	"I pray that out of his glorious riches he may strengthen you with power through his Spirit in your inner being, so that Christ may dwell in your hearts through faith. And I pray that you, being rooted and established in love, may have power, together with all the saints, to grasp how wide and long and high and deep is the love of Christ, and to know this love that surpasses knowledge— that you may be filled to the measure of all the fullness of God." (Ephesians 3:16–19)	"Christ dwells in my heart through faith, not because of what I can do." "I will never be able to grasp the extent of His love for me!"

LIES WE BELIEVE	SCRIPTURE	THE TRUTH ABOUT ME
"I need to love myself."	"After all, no one ever hated his own body, but he feeds and cares for it, just as Christ does the church—for we are members of his body." (Ephesians 5:29–30)	"I do love myself. I need to put on true humility."
"I am just a sinner. I can't help sinning."	"For we know that our old self was crucified with him so that the body of sin might be done away with, that we should no longer be slaves to sin—because anyone who has died has been freed from sin." (Romans 6:6–7) "You have been set free from sin and have become slaves to righteousness." (Romans 6:18)	"Because of Christ, I am no longer a slave to sin. I don't have to sin anymore."
"I deserve better than this." "I deserve to be happy." "I deserve to be loved."	"For the wages of sin is death, but the gift of God is eternal life in Christ Jesus our Lord." (Romans 6:23)	"What I really *deserve* is to die. But Christ died for me. Every day, everything is a gift."

LIES WE BELIEVE	SCRIPTURE	THE TRUTH ABOUT ME
"I will never get beyond my wicked past."	"Do you not know that the wicked will not inherit the kingdom of God? Do not be deceived: Neither the sexually immoral nor idolaters nor adulterers nor male prostitutes nor homo-sexual offenders nor thieves nor the greedy nor drunkards nor slanderers nor swindlers will inherit the kingdom of God. And that is what some of you were. But you were washed, you were sanctified, you were justified in the name of the Lord Jesus Christ and by the Spirit of our God." (1 Corinthians 6:9–11)	"It doesn't matter what I have done in my past. Because of Jesus Christ, I have been washed. I have been sanctified. I have been justified."
"God cannot forget the extent of my sin."	"Therefore, there is now no condemnation for those who are in Christ Jesus, because through Christ Jesus the law of the Spirit of life set me free from the law of sin and death." (Romans 8:1–2)	"God does not condemn me. I am free from the law of sin and death."

LIES WE BELIEVE	SCRIPTURE	THE TRUTH ABOUT ME
"To be a good Christian, I must suffer. I must go without things that I want and need."	"Taste and see that the LORD is good; blessed is the man who takes refuge in him. Fear the LORD, you his saints, for those who fear him lack nothing. The lions may grow weak and hungry, but those who seek the LORD lack no good thing." (Psalm 34:8–10)	"If I trust in God, I will lack nothing. If I seek Him, I will lack no good thing."
"I can't help but sin. I have no self-control."	"In the same way, count yourselves dead to sin but alive to God in Christ Jesus. Therefore do not let sin reign in your mortal body so that you obey its evil desires. Do not offer the parts of your body to sin, as instruments of wickedness, but rather offer yourselves to God, as those who have been brought from death to life; and offer the parts of your body to him as instruments of righteousness. For sin shall not be your master, because you are not under law, but under grace." (Romans 6:11–14)	"Because of God's grace, sin is no longer my master! I do not *have* to sin anymore."

LIES WE BELIEVE	SCRIPTURE	THE TRUTH ABOUT ME
"No one knows what I am going through."	"No temptation has seized you except what is common to man. And God is faithful; he will not let you be tempted beyond what you can bear. But when you are tempted, he will also provide a way out so that you can stand up under it." (1 Corinthians 10:13)	"This situation has happened to countless people before me. It is not new to God!"
"I can't take it anymore!"	"No temptation has seized you except what is common to man. And God is faithful; he will not let you be tempted beyond what you can bear. But when you are tempted, he will also provide a way out so that you can stand up under it." (1 Corinthians 10:13)	"God will not let me be tempted beyond what He knows I can handle. He will provide a way out."
"I can't do this."	"I can do everything through him who gives me strength." (Philippians 4:13)	"I *can* do this. God gives me strength."

The apostle Paul knew he would not live much longer. He chose Timothy to carry on his work of leading the early church. This would be like Billy Graham asking me to take over the Billy Graham Evangelistic Association and his Crusade ministry. Timothy thought to himself, "Who am I? I'm just a kid. People won't accept me as a leader because I am so young. I do not have what it takes to lead this enormous ministry. Paul has finally gone over the edge." Negative, lying self-talk. The truth was that Timothy was not only Paul's choice for the job, he was God's choice. God can use anyone to achieve His goals.

Or think about Abraham and Sarah. The couple had grown gray, never having had any children. God appeared to Abraham when he was ninety-nine years old and said that Sarah, although now eighty-nine, would conceive and bear a son. When Sarah overheard this, she snickered skeptically. "I am nothing but an old, wrinkling, shriveled-up woman. I did not have the biology to have a child when I was in my childbearing years, and I certainly don't have what it takes now!" Negative, lying self-talk. The truth was that Sarah would conceive a child and God's promise would be realized.

Or how about Moses? God appeared to him in a flaming bush. He informed Moses that he would deliver God's people from Pharaoh's oppression. Moses' reply was, "I am not all that bright, really. I am not eloquent enough for this job, and I'm not much to look at." Negative, lying self-talk. The truth was that God chose Moses. Moses' obedience was all that was required.

In all three of these biblical examples, the individuals' spiritual, physical, or emotional limitations had absolutely no bearing on their ability to fulfill God's plan. All that was really required of Timothy, Sarah, and Moses was to trust God and be obedient.

SUMMARY

Ladies, we need to identify those lies in our lives by which Satan holds us in shackles. We must take those thoughts captive and renew our minds by believing what *God* says about us and obeying Him.

Only then will we really be able to pass a blessing on to others. Only then will our hearts be free of pride, false humility, and low self-esteem. Only then will we stop being preoccupied with ourselves. Only then will our hearts and our words reflect thoughts that are excellent and praiseworthy:

> *Finally, brothers, whatever is true, whatever is noble, whatever is right, whatever is pure, whatever is lovely, whatever is admirable—if anything is excellent or praiseworthy—think about such things.*
> Philippians 4:8

Think about such things!

What a Beauty!

From the Inside Out

· · · · · · · · · · · · · · · ·

Your adornment must not be merely external—braiding
the hair, and wearing gold jewelry, or putting on dresses;
but let it be the hidden person of the heart, with the
imperishable quality of a gentle and quiet spirit, which is
precious in the sight of God.

1 PETER 3:3–4 (NASB)

Most people of a certain age have strong opinions about the 1980s. It was a strange decade of mostly mediocre music and apathetic social convictions, compared with its predecessors. The '80s accelerated an American obsession with material possessions and physical beauty.

The preoccupation with appearance included an odd, fickle fascination for fashion. In the '60s and '70s, there seemed to have been a rebellion against mainstream fashion. Some women wore long, straight hair and went for a natural look without makeup. Tie-dyed T-shirts and ragged bell-bottom jeans were acceptably chic.

The '80s, however, were a stark contrast. Style veered between the preppy look one day and *Flashdance* the next. Monday it was penny loafers, argyle socks, khaki slacks, and starched, pink oxford shirts buttoned all the way up with carefully knotted silk bows tied at the collar. Tuesday it was bulky knitted leg warmers over skin-tight leggings, torn-up sweatshirts, and at least one exposed shoulder. It was like a crazy scramble of rabid Brooks Brothers and Madonna-does-*Desperately Seeking Susan.* Dogs and cats living together!

In the 1980s, hair was permed to a precise frizz with "rooster" bangs standing vertically at attention. Not since early Mary Tyler Moore had hairspray manufacturers' stock been so bullish.

Then came the cosmetics craze. Mary Kay and Color-Me-Beautiful had women being made over in droves. We carried our color swatches in our handbags. "Oh, no. I couldn't possibly wear orange. I am a summer."

I aspired to wear eye shadow like Donna Mills, who played Abby on *Knots Landing,* a television drama. She looked like a femme fatale. I looked like a cross between a raccoon and the Lone Ranger gone bad. I would never have considered leaving the house without perfectly applied lipstick brushed on over matching lip liner and coordinating fingernails and toenails. Women were decked out to the nines at the corner market. (Today, I am lucky if I wear lipstick twice a week. Does Chapstick count? And nail polish—let's not go there.)

By the '90s, life for me revolved around the finest, perfectly tailored business suits I could afford and straight, flawless hair. Women wore basic black and classic beige and thankfully less makeup. Physical beauty was still of catastrophic significance. It was "simple yet sophisticated." Bright colors and sequins were shunned.

As the millennium arrived, womankind (and frightening enough, mankind as well) had found her fountain of youth. We are endlessly bleaching our teeth to a blinding white. We have bovine botulism (Botox) shot into unsightly wrinkles (or areas where there might be a wrinkle someday). Collagen is injected into lips like foam filling overstuffed pillows. Women's breasts are either enlarged or reduced on a whim, while cellulite is vacuumed away like yesterday's fireplace soot. Beauty is ever as critical as in the past twenty years, becoming more sought after thanks to technological advances and accessibility.

Is it just me, or does it seem that this obsession over allure has gotten out of hand?

Peter writes to the women of the early church that our adornment must not be merely external but the hidden person of the heart. He reminds women that external beauty is temporary, but internal beauty is imperishable:

> *Your adornment must not be merely external—braiding the hair, and wearing gold jewelry, or putting on dresses; but let it be the hidden person of the heart, with the imperishable quality of a gentle and quiet spirit, which is precious in the sight of God.*
>
> 1 Peter 3:3–4 (NASB)

I was brought up hearing this teaching summarized, "Beauty is as beauty does." "You are beautiful on the inside. That's what matters." Still, I discounted this message for almost thirty years. "I don't care what the Bible says, the way I look is the most important thing!" "That was then, this is now." "Sure, these shoes are uncomfortable, but they look good. That's all that counts." I just could not reconcile the thought that internal beauty was more important than external attractiveness with the current cultural craze for comeliness. No person could actually *see* my heart. No one would ever know if my spirit was resplendent. I figured I could dress up the outside and *act* the rest.

Then I ran across a verse that kicked the wind right out of my sails: "For the mouth speaks out of that which fills the heart" (Matthew 12:34 NASB). I thought, "That can't be saying what I think it's saying." So I checked the cross-reference, which was conveniently only a few pages over: "But the things that come out of the mouth come from the heart, and these make a man 'unclean'" (15:18). Well, since I believe that the Bible is 100 percent truth—my "dress up the outside" theory was blown to smithereens. Others *could* see that my heart was ugly (or rather, *hear* that it was ugly).

I had spent an overabundance of time, effort, and money meticulously wrapping up a lumpy, dingy scrap of coal. Instead, I should have been refining that coal into a diamond by cleaning up my heart. I suddenly felt an overwhelming sense of urgency to communicate this truth to others.

While speaking to a Christian women's group, I shared an illustration of the concept of inner beauty versus outer beauty. A precious six-year-old girl named Abigail was my assistant. I asked her who she believed to be the most beautiful woman in the entire world.

After much deep, face-twisting thought, she answered, "Britney Spears."

I said, "Alrighty then. We are going to pretend that I am Britney Spears."

(At this point Abigail innocently interjected, "You look like Britney Spears." To which I replied, "I love you. You are my new best friend.")

"Okay, new-best-friend Abigail, we are going to pretend that you are at the mall with your mom and you see me, Britney Spears. Since you think I, Britney Spears, am really cool, why don't you come over, introduce yourself to me, and say hello."

Abigail timidly tiptoed up to me and tapped me on the arm. "Hi, I'm Abigail."

"Britney" responded warmly, "Hi, Abigail. How are you today, sweetheart? You are such a pretty girl with such a pretty name. Thank you for coming over to say hello to me. You made my day!"

Then I (Rhonda) asked the audience and Abigail, "So what do you think of Britney Spears now? She is pretty neat, huh? She is really as beautiful as you thought she would be, isn't she? Now, let's try the same scenario once more."

Again, Abigail quietly approached me and tapped me on the arm. "Hi, I'm Abigail."

"Britney" bristled. "Can't you people just leave me alone? Why would you think I would want to be bothered by the likes of you? Just go away."

After I reassured Abigail that I was just pretending and that I thought she was absolutely delightful, I asked the audience again, "So, now, what do you think of Miss Britney Spears?"

I physically saw the lights go on in the faces of the women, young and old, in that room. "That Britney Spears is not so beautiful, is she? The geography didn't change. The characters didn't change. The only difference was the script. Britney's response— her words—was what defined how beautiful she really was in your eyes."

Does that help you perceive that beauty is truly a heart issue? "You can't solve your heart problem . . . just by cleaning up your speech."[1] I am here to tell you today, though, that you *can* solve your speech problem by cleaning up your heart.

A PLAN TO BEAUTIFY YOUR HEART

In chapter 1 we discussed how to achieve a Christ-centered heart. A beautiful heart and a Christ-centered heart are indistinguishable. Thus, the recipe is the same:

> *I seek you with all my heart;*
> *do not let me stray from your commands.*
> *I have hidden your word in my heart*
> *that I might not sin against you.*
> *Praise be to you, O LORD;*
> *teach me your decrees.*
>
> Psalm 119:10–12

1. Seek God through genuine prayer for a righteous heart.

2. Fill your heart with God's Word.

3. Train yourself in righteousness by learning God's decrees.

Now, are you ready to make a personal plan? In order to achieve any goal successfully, you must have a vision (Proverbs 29:18). Without a vision or plan, you will most likely never accomplish your objectives in life, because you will have neither a destination nor a way to get there.

To fashion a plan for beautifying your heart, first determine the areas in which you experience the greatest challenge and thus the areas that require the most urgent attention. Your *goal* will be to beautify your heart in those areas, and your *objectives* will be to render the areas of failure obsolete. Write out a strategy for accomplishing these objectives by incorporating Scripture memory, Bible study (group and/or personal), and prayer into your daily life. Determine that you will wholeheartedly seek God.

Use a table like the one below to help capture your harmful thoughts and patterns. Find Scripture (truth) that counters each weakness. Then develop a simple, one-sentence virtuous thought that will supersede the original problem thought and/or action.

A SAMPLE HEART BEAUTIFICATION PLAN

PROBLEM	TRUTH	REMEDY
Anger, Yelling	"My dear brothers, take note of this: Everyone should be quick to listen, slow to speak and slow to become angry, for man's anger does not bring about the righteous life that God desires." (James 1:19–20)	If I feel angry, I should take a moment to slow down (count to ten) and cool off before I speak.

PROBLEM	TRUTH	REMEDY
Complaining	"Trust in the LORD with all your heart and lean not on your own understanding; in all your ways acknowledge him, and he will make your paths straight." (Proverbs 3:5–6)	Trust God to meet my needs.
Cursing	"Out of the same mouth come praise and cursing. My brothers, this should not be." (James 3:10)	Stop cursing. Start blessing instead.
Gossiping	"A gossip betrays a confidence, but a trustworthy man keeps a secret." (Proverbs 11:13)	Be trustworthy.

I recommend writing the Scripture and the remedying thought on a note card that you can use for Scripture memory. Read the verse and/or the thought aloud five to twenty times to firmly establish it in your heart and mind. Review is how the psalmist hid God's Word in his heart:

> *With my lips I recount*
> *all the laws that come from your mouth.*
> Psalm 119:13

THE BEAUTIFUL WOMAN IN OTHERS' WORDS

A wise and worthy woman is characterized by kind words. She always communicates with grace. Here are some words others have to say about this kind of woman:

She opens her mouth and speaks wisdom. Kindness is the grace of her lips. She is wise and intelligent and highly cultured in mind and manners. She is graceful and even-tempered in all her ways.

—FINIS JENNINGS DAKE[2]

She is neither sullenly silent, nor full of impertinent talk, but speaks discreetly and piously, as occasion offers. . . .

Her speeches are guided by wisdom and grace, and not by inordinate passions. And this practice is called a law in her tongue, because it is constant and customary, and proceeds from an inward and powerful principle of true wisdom.

—JOHN WESLEY[3]

She openeth her mouth in wisdom.—[The writer of Proverbs 31]
1. She is wise and intelligent; she has not neglected the cultivation of her mind.
2. She is amiable in her carriage, full of good nature, well tempered, and conciliating in her manners and address.

In her tongue is the law of kindness.—This is the most distinguishing excellence of this woman. . . . This woman, with all her eminence and excellence, was of a meek and quiet spirit. Blessed woman!

—ADAM CLARKE[4]

I really like that phrase, *"In her tongue is the law of kindness—This is the most distinguishing excellence of this woman."*

A woman who is wise is patient and kind.
She speaks the truth in love when words are hard to find.
She finds the good in others and offers words of praise.
Many are encouraged by her understanding ways.

She listens very carefully, with confidence she speaks.
Finding truth and knowledge is something that she seeks. . . .

She doesn't care for gossip or believe in foolish lies
For she's a godly woman, she's a woman who is wise.

—CRYSTAL BOWMAN[5]

As you close this book, I pray that you will carefully ponder the ideas you have read. My desire is that this book will give you a new vision for how God's Word is real and alive for us today, and that you have gained insight into how biblical principles are relevant to our everyday needs in this twenty-first century.

I write this believing that as you apply these principles, you will begin to realize victory where you once experienced failure. Day by day, step by step, you will be transformed into that worthy woman of Proverbs 31. And others will say of you:

> *She opens her mouth in wisdom,*
> *And the teaching of kindness is on her tongue.*
>   Proverbs 31:26 (NASB)

Notes

Chapter 1: Where Did That Come From?

1. J. Lee Grady, *10 Lies the Church Tells Women* (Lake Mary, Fla.: Creation House, 2000), 129.
2. Martha Peace, *The Excellent Wife* (Bemidji, Minn.: Focus Publishing, 1999), 23.

Chapter 2: Was That the Wrong Thing to Say?

1. *Merriam-Webster's Collegiate Dictionary*, 10th ed., see "complain."
2. Ibid., see "grumble."
3. John E. Hartley, "Murmur," in *The International Standard Bible Encyclopedia*, rev. ed., vol. 3, gen. ed. Geoffrey W. Bromiley (1986; reprint, Grand Rapids: Eerdmans, 1990), 436.
4. *Webster's*, see "bitter."
5. Nigel Nicholson, "The New Word on Gossip," *Psychology Today*, June 2001, 41–45.
6. *Webster's*, see "slander."

Chapter 3: I'm Speechless

1. Johnson Oatman Jr., "Count Your Blessings," in *Songs for Young People,* by Edwin Excell (Chicago,1897). As found at www.cyberhymnal.org, December 31, 2002.
2. *Merriam-Webster's Collegiate Dictionary,* 10th ed., see "forbearance."
3. Jules Asner, "Will Smith Revealed," *Revealed with Jules Asner,* on E! Entertainment Television, 2002.

Chapter 4: Maybe Nobody Heard That

1. E. B. White, *Charlotte's Web* (New York: Harper Collins, 1952), 138–40.
2. David Martin, "Secretary of War," *60 Minutes II,* CBS News, 21 November 2001.

Chapter 5: Well, It's the Truth!

1. *Alanis for Real,* Oxygen network, 18 April 2000.
2. *Merriam-Webster's Collegiate Dictionary,* 10th ed., see "truth."
3. James Strong, *Strong's Universal Subject Guide to the Bible* (Nashville: Thomas Nelson, 1990), 205.
4. Strong, *Hebrew Dictionary of the Old Testament* (Nashville: Thomas Nelson, 1990), *emeth,* 14.
5. Ibid., *aman,* 14.
6. Ibid., *emunah,* 14.
7. Ibid., *qosht,* 105.
8. Ibid., *emun,* 14.
9. Ibid., *amanah,* 14.
10. *Webster's,* see "stability."
11. Ibid., see "permanent."
12. Ibid., see "firm."

Chapter 6: I *Had* to Say Something!

1. Louis Erdrich, as quoted in *1st Person: Maya Angelou,* www.HoustonChronicle.com, Michelle Buzgon/KRT.
2. Maya Angelou, *A Song Flung up to Heaven* (New York: Random House, 2002), 18.
3. Angelou, "Interview with Maya Angelou," *Oprah,* April 2002.
4. www.QuoteWorld.org.
5. Meg Kissinger, "Screech! Wham! Beep! Sssssssssshhh!," *Milwaukee Journal Sentinel,* 19 March 2001. (JSOnline), 4.
6. Ibid., 2.

Chapter 7: I've Told You Time and Time Again

1. James Strong, *Hebrew Dictionary of the Old Testament* (Nashville: Thomas Nelson, 1990), 56, 62.
2. See 1 Samuel 18:20–27; 19:11–17; 2 Samuel 3:13–16; 6:16–23.

Chapter 8: God Bless You

1. Gary Chapman, *The Five Love Languages* (Chicago: Northfield, 1995), 38.
2. Ibid., 42.
3. Marilyn Elias, "Teens Do Better When Dads Are More Involved," *USA Today,* 22 August 1996, sec. D, 1.

Chapter 9: Bless Me?

1. Joe Kolezynski, "Belief, Self-Talk and Performance Enhancement," *Selfhelp Magazine,* 31 August 1998, at http://www.shpm.com/articles/sports/selftalk.html.
2. Ibid.
3. Kay Arthur, *Lord, Heal My Hurts* (Sisters, Ore.: Multnomah, 1989), 127.
4. Beth Moore, *Breaking Free* (Nashville: Broadman and Holman, 2000), 238.
5. Martha Peace, *The Excellent Wife* (Bemidji, Minn.: Focus Publishing, 1999), 251.
6. Bruce Narramore and Elizabeth Skoglund, the brochure "Building Biblical Self-Esteem" (Arcadia, Calif.: Narramore Christian Foundation, 2001).
7. Stacy Colino, "Six Ways To Boost Your Self-Confidence," *Lifetime Online* (New York: Lifetime Entertainment Services, 2002).
8. Kolezynski, "Belief, Self-Talk."

Chapter 10: What a Beauty!

1. Bruce B. Barton, *Life Application Bible Notes* (Wheaton, Ill.: Tyndale, 1991), 1674.
2. Finis Jennings Dake, *Dake Annotated Reference Bible* (Lawrenceville, Ga.: Dake Publishing, 1996), 666.
3. *Wesley's Commentary.* Electronic text and markup copyright 1999 by Ephiphany Software. Note for Proverbs 31:26.
4. *Adam Clarke's Commentary.* Electronic text and markup copyright 1999 by Epiphany Software. Note for Proverbs 31:26.
5. Crystal Bowman, "A Woman Who Is Wise," in *Meditations for Moms* (Grand Rapids: Baker, 2001), 127.

Scripture Index

S INCE 1894, Moody Publishers has been dedicated to equip and motivate people to advance the cause of Christ by publishing evangelical Christian literature and other media for all ages, around the world. Because we are a ministry of the Moody Bible Institute of Chicago, a portion of the proceeds from the sale of this book go to train the next generation of Christian leaders.

If we may serve you in any way in your spiritual journey toward understanding Christ and the Christian life, please contact us at www.moodypublishers.com.

"All Scripture is God-breathed and is useful for teaching, rebuking, correcting and training in righteousness, so that the man of God may be thoroughly equipped for every good work."
—*2 TIMOTHY 3:16, 17*

MOODY
PUBLISHERS

THE NAME YOU CAN TRUST®

Words Begin in Our Hearts Team

Acquiring Editor:
Elsa Mazon

Copy Editor:
Wendy Peterson

Back Cover Copy:
Julie Allyson-Ieron, Joy Media

Cover Design:
Ragont Design

Interior Design:
Ragont Design

Printing and Binding:
Versa Press Incorporated

The typeface for the text of this book is
Meridien